Praise for Barbara Johnson

"Only heaven knows how many people have been lifted out of the doldrums and placed on higher ground both emotionally and spiritually because of the wit and the spiritual depth of Barbara Johnson. What a great lady!"

— Tony Campolo,
   Author and Speaker

"Barb's sterling heart and character glisten with Christ's beauty, and her humor keeps a smile on all of our hearts."

— Patsy Clairmont, Speaker, Women of Faith,
   Author, *I Grew Up Little*

"I have never responded well to anyone trying to tell me to 'Be Happy.' I didn't want to deny the truth of my trials or fake joy for any reason. Then I met Barbara Johnson. I heard her story, watched the way she lived, neither denying trials nor faking joy, and I thought, I'm listening . . . this woman can tell me anything she wants."

— Nicole Johnson, Dramatist, Women of Faith,
   Author, *Fresh-Brewed Life*

"Barbara Johnson has walked through the darkness holding on to the hand of God, and her life has become a brilliant light and comfort to millions around the world."

— Sheila Walsh, Speaker, Women of Faith,
   Author, *All That Really Matters*

"I will forever be grateful to Barbara for how she h~ ~ ~ use her. . . . Her life loves louder than her words ~ ~ am forever blessed and grateful for her ro^~

— Stephen Arterburn, Founder, ~
   Co-Host, *New Life Live!* radio p~

"Over a decade ago I went into a bookstore to ask for an inspirational book that would lift my spirits. The storeowner went immediately to Barbara Johnson's book, Stick a Geranium in Your Hat and Be Happy. I read the book and fell in love with this wacky woman. Watching Barbara go through her many trials has given me the image of what faith in God, trust in God, the love of God, and hope in God are from one who lives it.

— Thelma Wells, President, A Woman of God Ministries,
   Speaker, Women of Faith

"Barbara Johnson is in a league of her own. She's a slice of Lucille Ball, a cup of Erma Bombeck, a scoop of June Cleaver, and a gallon of Jesus. Barbara's words have touched more hearts and healed more hurts than any female author of our time. I am so honored and humbled to call her friend."

— Kathy Troccoli, Singer,
   Author (with Dee Brestin), *Falling in Love with Jesus,*
   Speaker, Women of Faith

"Barbara Johnson is one of those rare gems who makes us laugh at the unlaughable at just the right moment in time to turn unbearable tragedy into triumph. She has lifted the broken spirits of countless people across the world with her writing, her talks, her personal calls, and her letters. What a marvelous accomplishment it is that over a million people have read her words of wisdom, humor, and inspiration in this one book alone. I consider it an honor to know Barbara as my dear friend."

— Sam Butcher,
   Artist and Creator of Precious Moments

Stick a
Geranium in
Your Hat and
Be Happy!

Other Books by Barbara Johnson

Pain Is Inevitable but Misery Is Optional

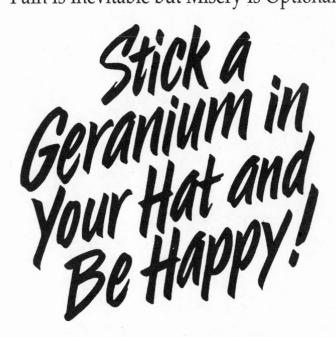

Stick a Geranium in Your Hat and Be Happy!

With a New Preface

Barbara Johnson

THOMAS NELSON
Since 1798

NASHVILLE   DALLAS   MEXICO CITY   RIO DE JANEIRO   BEIJING

Published in Nashville, TN, by Thomas Nelson. Thomas Nelson is a trademark of Thomas Nelson, Inc.

Thomas Nelson, Inc. titles may be purchased in bulk for educational, business, fundraising, or sales promotional use. For information, please email SpecialMarkets@ThomasNelson.com.

Scripture quotations used in this book are from the following sources:

The King James Version of the Bible (KJV).

The Holy Bible, New International Version (NIV). Copyright © 1973, 1978, 1984 International Bible Society. Used by permission of Zondervan Bible Publishers.

The New King James Version (NKJV). Copyright © 1979, 1980, 1982, Thomas Nelson, Inc., Publisher.

The Revised Standard Version of the Bible (RSV), copyrighted 1946, 1952, © 1971, 1973 by the Division of Christian Education of the National Council of the Churches of Christ in the U.S.A. Used by permission.

The Living Bible (TLB), copyright 1971 by Tyndale House Publishers, Wheaton, IL. Used by permission.

Selected poems are reprinted with permission from Ruth Harms Calkin's books *Lord, You Love to Say Yes* © 1976; *Lord, I Keep Running Back to You* © 1979; and *Lord, It Keeps Happening and Happening* © 1984. All rights reserved.

C. Austin Miles, "The World's Greatest Need," from *A Little More and a Little Less.* Copyright 1939, © Renewed 1967 by The Rodeheaver Co. (a division of Word, Inc.). All rights reserved. International copyright secured. Used by permission.

"She waited for the call that never came" copyright © 1977 Ruth Bell Graham. Used by permission of World Wide Publications.

"The Porch Light" and "Security Blanket" © 2003 Ann Luna. Used by permission of Ann Luna.

Robert E. Maner, "Tunnel Walking," from *Herald of Holiness.* Used by permission of Nazarene Publishing House.

"He'll See Them Home" used by permission of Joyce Henning.

Many of the quips, quotes, and jokes in this volume have been contributed as unidentified clippings by the author's many friends, and although we have diligently tried to identify the material's origin, doing so was sometimes impossible. For items that are tagged "source unknown" or where no source is named, the writer is not known, and the author claims no rights or ownership.

Library of Congress Cataloging-in-Publication Data

Johnson, Barbara (Barbara E.)
    Stick a geranium in your hat and be happy! / Barbara Johnson.
        p. cm.
    ISBN-10: 0-8499-4479-1
    ISBN-13: 978-0-8499-4479-6
        1. Mothers—Prayer-books and devotions—English. I. Title.
    BV4847.J63
    248.8'431—dc20

89–29511
CIP

Printed in the United States of America

08 09 10 11 RRD 12 11 10

TO DAVID,*

my son, who honors me by calling me his best friend.
His experiences blend with mine to be a lighthouse
for parents who are struggling to find some hope
for their broken dreams.

*There is hope for your future, says the LORD,
and your children shall come back
to their own country.*
—*Jeremiah 31:17, RSV*

---

*Called "Larry" in this book, as well as in *Where Does a Mother Go to Resign?*
(Bethany 1979) and *Fresh Elastic for Stretched-Out Moms* (Revell 1986).

CONTENTS

---

*Ashleigh Brilliant, Pot-Shots No. 519, © Brilliant Enterprises 1974. Used by permission

ACKNOWLEDGMENTS

My appreciation and thanks to the many people who have so graciously shared with me stories, poems, letters, and other material that appears in this book. Bless you for the encouragement and joy you spread!

I have made diligent effort to locate the author and source of the material I quote in this book; however, because I receive clippings, handwritten notes, church bulletins, and all sorts of other items from friends and readers all over the world, I often have no way of identifying the original source. To those unknown writers whose words appear here as "source unknown," I say thank you for sharing your wonderful inspiration and wit.

Special acknowledgment and my sincere thanks also go to the following individuals and companies:

Ashleigh Brilliant for his permission to use Ashleigh Brilliant Epigrams, Pot-Shots, and Brilliant Thoughts (Brilliant Enterprises, 117 West Valerio St., Santa Barbara, CA 93101).

Shannon Johnson, my daughter-in-love, for her sketches and creative suggestions that ultimately led to the drawings used in this book.

And thanks to these writers and organizations for permission to use selected poems:

Ruth Harms Calkin for poems from her books *Lord, I Keep Running Back to You; Lord, You Love to Say Yes;* and *Lord, It Keeps Happening and Happening.*

Nazarene Publishing House for Robert E. Maner's poem, "Tunnel Walking," from *Herald of Holiness.*

The C. Austin Miles poem "The World's Greatest Need," from *A Little More and a Little Less*, The Rodeheaver Co. (a division of Word, Inc.).

Joyce Henning for permission to use the poem "He'll See Them Home."

Minnie Lee Dear for permission to use her mother, Pearl Waddell's, poem, "I'm Fine."

World Wide Publications for Ruth Bell Graham's poem "She Waited for the Call That Never Came."

2004 Preface

The "book table girls" used to play a little game when we traveled together during my years of touring the country with the Women of Faith Conference. In each different city where the conference was held, they noted the time when the first woman came up to my book table, laid her hand on the volume with the pink cover, and said, "This book saved my life!" The earliest recorded time, I believe, was in Cincinnati at 4:15 P.M. more than an hour before the doors even opened for the Friday night session. The woman was one of the workers in the arena, and she stopped by as we were setting up to let us know what an impact *Geranium,* as we call it, had made on her life after her daughter had been killed in a car crash.

I'd like to say I planned all along that this book would sell a million copies, be translated into dozens of languages around the world, and still be going strong fourteen years later. After all, it's every author's dream. But the truth is, what I really wanted to do was to help that one unknown woman in Cincinnati who had lost a child—as well as an unknown, brokenhearted mother in Portland who had just found out her child was homosexual. I wanted to reach out, one to one, heart to heart, to help that one freshly hurt mother who felt as though no one could possibly understand the depth of her despair.

Well, sister, I understand! I've seen the view from the edge of the abyss. I have been a brokenhearted woman—I still am—and I know that in our pain we hurting parents turn to many different comforters—friends, pastors, counselors, support groups. All of them can be valuable and effective. But what worked best for many of us was simply another mother who had been through heartache herself and who came alongside us to cry with us, to model a firm grip on God's loving promises, and then to gently nudge us back to normalcy, a place we thought we'd never see again.

One woman told me, "Barbara, you taught me to laugh again, even though my heart is breaking."

That was my goal in writing *Stick a Geranium in Your Hat and Be Happy*: to help one hurting mother learn to laugh again when she never dreamed that was possible. I'm so blessed to know that thousands and thousands of those hurting mothers—dads, too—have let me come alongside them through the pages of this book. Many of them have returned the favor by sharing their back-from-the-brink stories with me. At one Women of Faith conference, the mother of a gay child thumped the stack of *Geraniums*, and proclaimed, "This book saved my daughter's life!"

This was a slightly different slant on the usual statement, so I was curious. "Oh, your *daughter* read my book?" I asked.

"No," the woman answered. "*I* read it. And it kept me from killing her."

In one city a young *man* came up to the book table. This was certainly unusual at a Women of Faith conference! The young man said he had just been released from prison. He was gay, HIV-positive, and he'd been imprisoned for dealing drugs. All his adult life his mother had begged him to return to God and to leave behind the destructive lifestyle he had sunk into. "She prayed for me all the time," he said, "but I turned my back on everything she tried to tell me."

So he ended up in prison, and to pass the time, he read the books in the prison library. There weren't many, and he read them *all*, he said, except for one book that was obviously for women. It had a pink cover depicting a goofy-looking woman wearing a big hat with a geranium stuck in it. But boredom eventually won out, and one day he reluctantly borrowed that one last book he hadn't read.

A few days later he called his mother. "I finally get it, Mom," he told her. "I see what you've been trying to tell me.

God loves me. Even though I've wrecked my life, He still loves me."

"Oh, Honey, what happened?" the overjoyed mother asked.

"I read this book, Mom: *Stick a Geranium in Your Hat and Be Happy*. It's—"

"Oh, son, I've read it, too!"

The young man telling the story at the book table turned to the tiny woman standing beside him. "This is my mom," he said. "We bought tickets to the conference just so we could come and say thank you."

There have been many similar stories since *Geranium* was first published. I call them my boomerang blessings; I sent out my story hoping to help someone, and the help and encouragement have come bounding back to me a thousandfold.

Such blessings have been especially helpful to me in the last couple of years as I have battled cancer and said "good-bye for now" to my husband, Bill. Last summer, a few days before Bill went to be with the Lord, he and I were teasing each other about losing weight. He had lost several pounds due to his own battle with bone cancer. He said, "Well, I don't have to worry about it now, because in a few days I'll be wearing a new white robe."

When I jokingly asked him, "Do you think it'll be one-size-fits-all?" he answered, "Of course! That'll be the only kind we'll need up there!"

Despite the pain we were both experiencing, we were able, once again, to laugh together, just as we'd done in spite of all the heartache we'd shared over the years. I hope if you're hurting because of some whirlwind that's suddenly swept into your life and dumped you in the cesspool, that you will find both encouragement in my story, so that, despite hardships, you'll eventually find a way to laugh again. Most importantly, I hope my story can be your lifeline so that you can turn around someday and help someone else who's recently landed in the cesspool.

It's been an amazing experience to see how God has used

this little pink book as a conduit of His love. I've been tremendously blessed to be the goofy-looking, hat-wearing "Geranium Lady" on the cover.

Still joyful,

Barbara Johnson

1990 Preface

Can you just "STICK A GERANIUM IN YOUR HAT" and be happy?

I know you can, no matter what happens. We all have to endure troubles in life. Sometimes we may go along for a while with just common irritations and then, WHAM! A big problem hits, and we have a real valley experience. But I believe that you grow in the valleys because that's where all the fertilizer is.

In my first book, *Where Does a Mother Go to Resign?* (Bethany, 1979), I wrote about my own valley times: the terrible accident that left my husband blind and crippled for many months; the deaths of two sons, one in Vietnam and the other on a highway in the Yukon; and the homosexuality of another son who disappeared into the gay lifestyle for the better part of eleven years. I have learned to welcome the valley times because I have seen the growth in character that comes from them. And I have survived only by partaking of a steady diet of laughter, joy, and hope.

About four years ago, I was speaking at a Christian book-sellers function and decided to close my talk with a line from the new book I had just written entitled *Fresh Elastic for Stretched-Out Moms* (Revell, 1986). That line was: "Life isn't always what you want, but it's what you've got, so stick a geranium in your hat and be happy!" For some reason that thought clicked in the minds of my listeners, and they responded with a standing ovation, planting the seeds of another book to help hurting people.

And here it is!

We can choose to gather to our hearts the thorns of disappointment, failure, loneliness, and dismay due to our present situation, or we can gather the flowers of God's grace, unbounding love, abiding presence, and unmatched joy. I choose to gather the flowers, and I hope you will, too. SO, FIND YOURSELF A GERANIUM AND STICK IT IN YOUR HAT! If this book helps you decide you want the flowers and not the thorns of life, I will have accomplished my purpose.

Joyfully,

Barbara Johnson

1

Pain Is Inevitable, But Misery Is Optional*

LOST

*Dog with 3 legs,
blind in left eye, missing
right ear, tail broken, and
recently castrated. Answers
to the name of "Lucky."*

—Sign on Grocery Store Bulletin Board

After I spoke at a women's retreat recently, a darling gal rushed up to me saying, "Oh, Barb, you are just SO LUCKY! You have come through all your trials with so much joy and victory! Now you get to travel all over the country, be dressed up, and meet so many famous people and enjoy being a celebrity. You have really got it all together now!"

I laughed and told the lady that I didn't believe there was any such thing as luck for Christians. Luck doesn't come into our lives, but a lot of other things do.

Look at it this way: One family out of 500,000 lost a son in Vietnam . . . we are one of those families.

One family out of every 800 has a loved one killed by a drunk driver . . . we experienced that, too.

---

*The title of this chapter is an expression frequently used by Tim Hansel that I've found especially meaningful in my life.

Statistics say that one family out of every ten will have a homosexual child . . . we know all about that.

And recently I became part of another set of statistics, namely that out of every forty women over middle age, one will develop adult-onset diabetes.

Diabetes—A New Experience for Me

This is something that is brand-new in my life. Although it is considered milder than juvenile-onset, it carries with it all the life-threatening complications. I learned I had adult-onset diabetes during a simple physical examination. Up to that point, I had had no symptoms, no complaints, no warning signs. My doctor was dead serious when he explained to me the consequences of not following his orders, which seemed ridiculous to me at first.

My orders were to avoid stress, get plenty of rest, restrict intake of foods (eliminating all good stuff with sugar, of course), eat several small meals a day at specific times, and prick my finger daily to keep track of my blood glucose levels. (This lets me know if I'm maintaining good glucose control.) Then he finished by saying, "And because you're not the kind to accept that you have a chronic, debilitating disease, you must attend a support group for diabetic people."

"ME? ME, ATTEND A SUPPORT GROUP? *I LEAD* a support group! Why ever in the world would *I GO* to one?"

"Yes," he said, "otherwise you won't recognize the severity of it and will neglect taking care of yourself."

The following week found me dragging my feet as I entered a room full of diabetic sufferers at a local hospital conference room. As I looked around, I saw about forty people, and immediately I decided the doctor had selected the most devastated cases to present themselves that night, just for my benefit alone!

On my first visit I was considered a guest, so I didn't have to say anything, just observe. That was good because what I saw left me practically speechless anyway. One lady had gangrene and was to have her leg amputated soon. One man there had no feeling in his legs or feet. Another lady was blind from diabetes and also had other complications.

As the stories unfolded, it seemed that each one was more horrible than the previous one. Every complication of diabetes was described, and it seemed that of those present, they all had one or more of them to contend with. I could hardly wait to escape that meeting. What a hopeless group! Their future appeared bleak as they rehearsed the complications that could arise from this life-threatening disease.

The next week I was back in the doctor's office, pouring out to him how dreadful that diabetic support group was. "These people may need this, but I sure don't. Can't you tell me something GOOD to say tonight when it is my turn to share?"

"Well," he said, "having diabetes is like having carpenter ants in your body. You never know where they might attack . . . it could be the kidneys, the arteries, your vision, etc."

"That's hardly something encouraging that I could share!"

"Well, just pretend that the most upsetting relative you have has come to live with you for the rest of your life."

"That's another ZERO to share! But I have to speak at tonight's meeting, and I just have to say something positive to these poor, pitiful souls."

The doctor paused and then he smiled. "Well, knowing you, you'll think this is something good. One good thing about having diabetes is that you won't end up in a rest home because usually diabetics don't LIVE that long!"

"Oh, that's terrific news!" I said. "Who wants to end up in a rest home anyway? Besides, my husband, Bill, has just taken out some insurance with the American Association of Retired Persons that's supposed to cover any needs for a rest home. Now I can cancel my portion!"

I went home and joyfully instructed Bill to cancel my portion of that AARP rest home policy and then headed out for the hospital support group for diabetics meeting.

There they sat, just as they had the week before. No one had grown a new leg, and no miracles had happened since the last meeting. All of them just sat there in a circle, pouring out new complaints and new pains.

Finally it got to be my turn. I started out with my name and said that I was only at this meeting because my doctor said I HAD to come to at least two meetings, but I wouldn't be back after this one.

"My doctor told me recently that I have adult-onset diabetes and warned me about all the complications that go along with it unless I take proper care of myself. And even then I have no guarantee I'll escape them. But I was back to see him today, and he gave me some really terrific news!"

Every face in the group sort of brightened up, and I continued, "The doctor told me I don't have to worry about winding up in a rest home because diabetics usually don't live that long!"

At this point, I could see that they were about to fall off their chairs, but I had to continue telling them how exciting it is for me to know that as a Christian I have an ENDLESS HOPE, not a HOPELESS END. It seemed that the Lord wrapped me in so much love for these folks that it just poured out of me. I told them that my exit from earth would be my grandest entrance in heaven and that earth has no sorrow heaven cannot heal. My joy is in knowing that my future is in God's hands and that heaven is closer to me than long life in some rest home.

There Is Only One Thing You Can Control

I said a lot more, but the main thrust was that I chose to look at what seemed *good* to me rather than to anticipate all the gruesome complications that can happen at some point. Afterward, many in the group asked me questions about my ideas on life because, evidently, no one had shared anything encouraging with them before. I told them that pain is inevitable for all of us, but that we have an option as to how we react to the pain. It is no fun to suffer; in fact, it can be awful. We are all going to have pain, but *misery is optional.* We can decide how we will react to the pain that inevitably comes to us all.

Since learning that I have diabetes, I have read a dozen books and even watched some video tapes to learn all I could about how to cope with this chronic, debilitating disease. The most important thing I learned is that having a proper mental attitude works wonders. If you take care of yourself and do all the things that you must do to keep it in control so that it doesn't control you, you can live a happy, productive life.

I didn't want this disease, and I surely empathize with others who have endured it for many years, but I choose to do all I can to care for myself and enjoy each day that I am here. I constantly remind myself:

*THE ONLY THING YOU CAN REALLY
CONTROL IN THIS LIFE
IS YOUR OWN MENTAL ATTITUDE.*

Recently I was in Sacramento speaking for a women's retreat, and a cheerful, perky gal in a wheelchair volunteered to help me at the book table. Her name was Mary Jane. She only had one leg, and I wondered if diabetes might have claimed the other one. But she just whirled around in that wheelchair, getting change and doing a fabulous job of handling customers who wanted to buy my books.

We talked later, and Mary Jane told me that her leg had been amputated because of cancer. Then she began to laugh and told me that for years her doctor had been after her to lose weight. He had put her on diets, which were always unsuccessful, and when she finally went in for the leg amputation, she said from the operating table, "Now you be sure to weigh the leg so that you can remove that amount of weight from my chart!"

What an attitude! Her pain is inevitable, but she chooses to make her option something *other* than misery!

So does a man I met at the La Habra post office. You'll be reading a lot about that place because it seems I spend a lot of my life there. My license plate says SPATULA, and the other day when I pulled in to park at the post office, I noticed the plate on the car next to me said: "2 BUM NEZ." I thought, *That's so cute—the guy probably has arthritis or something.*

As I tore around the car with my arms full of tapes and books to mail, I called out, "Oh, I just LOVE your license plate!" Suddenly I saw that he didn't have any legs! Talk about hoof-and-mouth disease! Someone was helping him out of the car, but he put me at ease by saying, "I'm glad you like it. My wife said I should get one that said, "NO LEGS," but I would rather have folks get a chuckle out of it like you did than have them feel sorry for me."

Bill and I See Life Differently

I love that man's attitude because it illustrates so beautifully how pain is inevitable, but misery is optional. We cannot escape having pain in this life, but our choice is in how we react to it. For years I've been trying to convince Bill, my darling but melancholy husband, that how you look at life can either bring a sparkle of joy or a handful of gloom.

Recently we had car trouble and had to be towed from San Diego to our home, a distance of nearly 100 miles at a cost of about one dollar per mile. I had never even been in a tow truck before, and it was really fun sitting up so high and looking down at all the little cars whirring by. Being up so high, I could see everything perfectly, even our car attached behind. But Bill didn't think it was fun at all. He didn't think it was an adventure. He didn't think there was anything cheery about it.

Trying to lift his dark and depressing mood, I chirped loudly, "But think of all the gasoline we are saving!" For me, it was a new, fun experience. We probably would never ride that far in a tow truck again, so why not enjoy ourselves since we had to be doing it anyway? But Bill didn't see it that way. We often view life differently, Bill seeing the glass half empty while I see it brim full and running over.

One thing I love about Bill is that he always lets me be myself. In chapter 8, I'll explain how God put our personalities together to balance each other and to be a smoothly working team. Bill's steady, organized ways do much to make our ministry a success!

Twenty Dollars for Two Maple Bars?

A few years back—before diabetes and *really* having to watch my diet—Bill and I decided to work on our mutual weight problem by walking. So, at night we would walk to the Baskin-Robbins ice cream shop to have an ice cream cone night cap. And in the mornings we would walk to the Yum Yum Donut shop for our usual hot coffee and warm maple bars. On one particular morning, we had made it to Yum Yum's in record time, and I reached in my sweater pocket for the twenty dollar bill I had brought along. Bill didn't have his wallet with him, and I had left my purse at home because heavy purses aren't much good on brisk walks.

We ordered our usual, and when the girl brought it, I plunked my twenty down on the counter. She took my money and disappeared to the back room to get cream and more napkins. When she returned, she asked for two dollars and fifty cents. She didn't speak very distinct English, but she made it clear she expected money. And I told her she had just picked up my twenty dollar bill when she had gone out back for more cream.

It didn't make any difference. All she could keep saying was that we owed her two dollars and fifty cents, and she didn't seem to "understand" about the strange disappearance of my twenty dollar bill! By this time, people were coming in the door and standing in line, all waiting to order their coffee and donuts. Bill was getting annoyed with all this fumbling around and tried to come to my aid. After all, he had *seen* the girl pick up the twenty dollar bill I'd laid down. So had another lady who had been sitting near by.

I thought, *Who do you call at a time like this?* Bill suggested cleaning out the cash register and PROVING she had taken our money. I also thought of calling the police but decided against it. They might not believe us, and we couldn't prove we put the money on the counter.

Very much embarrassed, we took the coffee and maple bars

to a little table and sat down. I began planning on how we could leave if she still insisted we owed her money. We had no more money with us. And what if she called the police and said we couldn't pay her for what we ordered? Bill already had taken a bite out of his maple bar, and we couldn't return it . . .

I tried to appear unobtrusive, glancing at a newspaper lying on the seat next to me and reading the signs on the window, but Bill kept muttering loudly, saying things like, "This is the most expensive donut and coffee I've ever had—TWENTY DOLLARS FOR TWO MAPLE BARS AND COFFEE!"

We finished our maple bars and coffee and left without the girl trying to stop us. Bill kept yakking about it as we walked back home, wanting ME to call the main office of the Yum Yum Donut Shops and complain that they had taken our money. All the way back he fumed about paying twenty dollars for our small order. Suddenly I remembered that several years ago, in front of our church, I had FOUND a twenty dollar bill.

"Hey, Bill, remember when I found that twenty dollar bill a few years ago by our church?"

Bill didn't remember. But I told him, "Why not look at it this way? That was the same twenty dollar bill we lost today, so really we got the maple bars and coffee for FREE!"

Bill looked at me as if I were someone from outer space and continued being depressed about losing that much money. For a couple of weeks, his irritation over the whole episode left a heavy cloud over everything.

With his melancholy temperament, he harbored ill feelings. He didn't want to go back to the Yum Yum Donut Shop and preferred nourishing the idea that he had been done wrong. But I had decided I had more enjoyable things to do than worry about a lost twenty dollar bill, especially since, the way I looked at it, we really got the maple bars for free!

It Depends on How You Look at It

Now, I can't be sure of all the spiritual significance of the Yum Yum Donut Shop story, except to remember that the apostle Paul also believed that having joy or misery all depends on how you look at it. His advice was, "Whatever is true, whatever is noble, whatever is right, whatever is pure, whatever is lovely, whatever is admirable—if anything is excellent or praiseworthy—think about such things" (Philippians 4:8, NIV). And that's exactly what I did about the twenty dollar bill. I thought our experience was praiseworthy, but Bill felt we had been gypped out of our money.

So, it is all in how we choose to look at the circumstances. We can look for the flowers or the weeds. We can see the bright side or look for the clouds. Remember:

YOU CAN BE AS HAPPY AS YOU DECIDE TO BE.

How you look at things really can make the difference in setting the mood for the day. I found the following little story and put it in my newsletter, *The Love Line,* to help people see how they can enjoy their day, their week, and their year, even in the midst of tragedy.

The day had started out rotten. I overslept and was late for work. Everything that happened at the office contributed to my nervous frenzy. By the time I reached the bus stop for my homeward trip, my stomach was one big knot.

As usual, the bus was late—and jammed. I had to stand in the aisle. As the lurching vehicle pulled me in all directions, my gloom deepened.

Then I heard a deep voice from up front boom, "Beautiful day, isn't it?" Because of the crowd I could not see the man, but I could hear him as he continued to comment on the spring scenery, calling attention to each approaching landmark. This church. That park. This cemetery. That firehouse. Soon all the passengers were gazing out the windows. The man's enthusiasm was so contagious I found myself smiling for the first time that day.

We reached my stop. Maneuvering toward the door, I got a look at our "guide": a plump figure with a black beard, wearing dark glasses and carrying a thin white cane. Incredible! He was blind!

I stepped off the bus and, suddenly, all my built-up tensions drained away. God in His wisdom had sent a blind man to help me see—see that, though there are times when things go wrong, when all seems dark and dreary, it is still a beautiful world. Humming a tune, I raced up the steps to my apartment. I couldn't wait to greet my husband with "Beautiful day, isn't it?"

—Source Unknown

You Can Always Get a Fresh Start

I think every day should be a beautiful day—a fresh start. When I speak in seminars and workshops, I often take along a box of FRESH START soap as a visual aid to emphasize this point. At home I use FRESH START to wash clothes and JOY to wash dishes. They both remind me that you can always find joy in a new beginning. When I wash clothes in the morning, I say, "Thank you, Lord, for a fresh start—a day that isn't even messed up yet and a new beginning." I can even enjoy doing the laundry because I think about getting a fresh start.

I've never met Patricia Liba, but something she wrote about "The New Day" sums up exactly how I feel:

I woke up this morning to overcast skies, but the day was new . . . a *never-been-lived-before kind of day. I* took my shower and counted my blessings for the little things, like plenty of hot water and a brand new bar of soap. As I hummed an unrecognizable tune, I remembered how much I enjoyed and absorbed that old western movie last night, while munching on popcorn. I let my mind ramble further as I shampooed my hair and thought about our cozy, small, old home that contains just about every wonderful memory-maker ever known. No unpleasant memories here, although many of my possessions once belonged to now-gone loved ones. These knick-knacks give my life fuller meaning and their comfort and continuity stay with me as I go about my daily chores. I smiled to myself and I shut the water off, glad that once dried off and dressed, I would be . . . stepping briskly and happily into my *never-been-lived-before* day.

— Reprinted from
Sunshine Magazine

I think of Pat's words every time I take a shower in the morning. I use Dove soap and think of how the Holy Spirit cleanses us and refreshes us, making us clean inside and out. I'm looking at a new day—a day that nobody has messed up yet. Nothing has happened, and it's a whole brand-new day that I can enjoy. It's a day that hasn't been lived in, but I'm going to live it with gusto. I love the little sign on the desk of my friend who works at a mortuary:

> *ANY DAY ABOVE GROUND*
> *IS A GOOD ONE!*

I don't have all the answers to life, but I know Someone who does. I want to live as though Christ died yesterday, rose today, and is coming tomorrow.

Am I a Little Too Joyful?

Sometimes I meet people who think I'm a little too joyful—that I'm ducking reality and ignoring the painful facts of life. But I simply tell them I'm not ignoring the facts—I'm just looking at them and trying to find joy, not misery.

We all know there are 365 days in a year, but I believe there are only three days we should be concerned about dealing with correctly. And two of those days we can do nothing about—yesterday and tomorrow. Yesterday is a canceled check, and tomorrow is a promissory note. But today is cash, ready for us to spend in living, and that's why I say wake up and rejoice and take advantage of the FRESH START. There are no mistakes, nothing has happened, and nobody has goofed it up—we've got today! We've got another chance!

Now if you can go through a few days like that, pretty soon you've got a week and maybe even a month when you have rejoiced over every new day and not worried about the past. And if you're trusting in Christ, you surely don't have to worry about the future. I like the Bible's advice to "be beautiful inside, in your hearts, with the lasting charm of a gentle and quiet spirit which is so precious to God" (1 Peter 3:4, TLB).

That reminds me of a letter I got from a fantastic woman who has been through one of the longest periods of suffering I have ever known. She wrote a note to encourage me because she knows my story is ongoing, just as hers is. In her note, she said something I hope every reader of this book can grasp, learn, remember, and recall on those days when you feel drained and spent . . . completely washed out . . . when you think you cannot go on another day . . . when you want to resign and don't know where to go . . . when you really want to hang it all up and forget the whole thing. On days like that, remember this:

> We cannot let our burdens
> paralyze our progress.

How easy it is to just freeze with our finger on the panic button, trapped in our grief and heartache, unable to help anyone, even ourselves. So many of my phone calls reflect the paralysis that engulfs parents who are hurting when they first learn their kids are into drugs, the homosexual lifestyle, or some other mess. They are in the shock stage. The trauma is devastating. The hurt is such as they have never known. The pain is intense; they are fractured inside and think they will never be a complete person again. It is a "Humpty Dumpty" feeling, which they may have to learn to live with for a while.

Perhaps you, too, are going through this kind of experience. There are no pat answers, no simple ways to ease the pain, but *never let your burdens paralyze your progress.* Yes, you're hurting, along with hundreds and thousands of others who are hurting also. But progress will come to you as you reach out from under your load and try to lift the load of someone else. Try doing something for another person who also is straining with her burden. Love your way out of that paralyzed state, thaw the panic-button situation, and don't be immobilized any longer by your own burdens.

And that's why I wrote this book. I've already referred to the tragedies that I believe give me the credentials to share with you. I tell that story in my first book, *Where Does a*

Mother Go to Resign? I'll repeat it in abbreviated form in the next two chapters, sharing some things I didn't get into in the first book and giving some insights on what I learned as my husband, Bill, and I operated SPATULA, a special ministry designed to help scrape parents off the ceiling when they learned that they have a homosexual child or faced some other broken dream in their family. I also tried to speak wherever I could—in person or on TV or radio—to help encourage parents who were in real pain because their kids have disappointed them.

Life Gives You No Time to Rehearse

Once when I was talking with Al Sanders on one of his "Vox Pop" radio broadcasts, he quoted something from Ashleigh Brilliant that I often say: "My life is a performance for which I was never given any chance to rehearse."[1] Then he asked, "Why do you say that?"

I told him this: "Suddenly life has happened. I didn't have any chance to prepare for the four tragedies that hit our family over a period of nine years. But I believe that when I talk to you now, I have credentials because I've been in the pits. I've been through the tragedies, but now I've got a lot of joy. I want to inject that joy and humor and hope into the people who are listening."

Every day is so precious, we have no time to waste. Some days may bring pain, but we always have a choice between misery and joy. The secret is to live one day at a time and to make the right choices as you go along. Ralph Waldo Emerson was a wise thinker, and one of the best pieces of advice he ever gave the world was this:

> Finish every day and be done with it. You have done what you could. Some blunders and absurdities no doubt have crept in; forget them as soon as you can. Tomorrow is a new day; begin it well and serenely and with too high a spirit to be cumbered with your old nonsense. This day is all that is good and fair. It is too dear, with its hopes and invitations, to waste a moment on yesterdays.

A few weeks ago I was chatting on the phone with Dr. Walter Martin about some problems I was having getting books sent to Canada where I was to speak at a Bible conference. I had been in his Bible class for years, and he had written the introduction to my first book, *Where Does a Mother Go to Resign?* Over the years his tapes have also been such an encouragement to me. He gave me some pointers about how to solve the book-shipment problem, and then, since I knew he had diabetes, I shared with him that I, too, had been diagnosed as having diabetes. When l joked about our probably never having to end up in a rest home, he laughed and said, "That being the case, perhaps I should sell my interest in a rest home back east." We laughed some more, and I told him about this very book, which I was in the process of writing.

Ten days after our phone conversation, Dr. Walter Martin was singing praises around the throne of God. A sudden, unexplained heart attack, and he was gone! Life is so fragile for all of us. How important to make decisions that count for eternity! Eternity is waiting for all of us, but if we can accept the pain that comes in this life and choose to react positively, we can avoid misery. We always have the option to choose JOY!

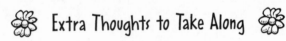 **Extra Thoughts to Take Along**

THE PIT

A man fell into a pit and couldn't get himself out.
A SUBJECTIVE person came along and said,
   "I feel for you, down there."
An OBJECTIVE person came along and said, "It's logical
   that someone would fall down there."
A PHARISEE said, "Only bad people fall into a pit."
A MATHEMATICIAN calculated how he fell into the pit.
A NEWS REPORTER wanted the exclusive story on his pit.
A FUNDAMENTALIST said, "You deserve your pit."
An IRS agent asked if he was paying taxes on the pit.
A SELF-PITYING person said, "You haven't seen any-
   thing until you've seen MY PIT!"

A CHARISMATIC said, "Just confess that you're not in
   a pit."
An OPTIMIST said, "Things could be worse."
A PESSIMIST said, "Things will get worse!"
JESUS, seeing the man, took him gently by the hand and
   LIFTED HIM OUT of the pit.

— Source Unknown

* * * *

Stress is when you wake up screaming . . . and realize you
haven't fallen asleep yet.

* * * *

It is as if we
are meant to be
wearing bifocals in
our attitude to life in

the world. We are to see
clearly the job at hand and do
it hard and well, but we are to
have long-distance vision as well so
that we can be aware of God's perspective and the relevance of His work in our lives.

— From an Ophthalmologist's
Newsletter

* * * *

RESOLUTIONS FOR AVOIDING MISERY

Choose to love—rather than hate.
Choose to smile—rather than frown.
Choose to build—rather than destroy.
Choose to persevere—rather than quit.
Choose to praise—rather than gossip.
Choose to heal—rather than wound.
Choose to give—rather than grasp.
Choose to act—rather than delay.
Choose to forgive—rather than curse.
Choose to pray—rather than despair.

— Source Unknown

* * * *

DON'T FORGET

Life is about 10 percent how you make it . . .
And 90 percent how you take it.

I Can Handle
Any Crisis—I'm a Mother

No matter how calmly you try to referee,
parenting will eventually produce bizarre behavior,
and I'm not talking about the kids. . . . You will find yourself
strolling down the road to the funny farm.

— Bill Cosby

Most of us mothers don't feel we deserve all the flowery verses and accolades that come to us on Mother's Day, but we know that this day is meaningful to our families. In the month of May, *The Love Line* newsletter is dedicated to moms, reminding them that:

IF IT WAS GOING TO BE EASY TO RAISE KIDS,
IT NEVER WOULD HAVE STARTED WITH
SOMETHING CALLED LABOR.

— Source Unknown

But that's what motherhood is—a labor of love. One of my favorite stories (and I have no idea where it came from originally) talks about how a mother's love outlasts everything. It seems an angel slipped out of heaven and spent the day roaming around the earth. As the sun was setting, he decided he wanted to take along some mementos of his visit. He noticed some lovely roses in a flower garden, plucked the rarest and most beautiful, and made a bouquet to take back to heaven.

Looking on a bit farther, he saw a beautiful little baby smiling into its mother's face. The baby's smile was even prettier than the bouquet of roses, so he took that, too. He was about to leave when he saw the mother's love pouring out like a gushing river toward the little baby in the cradle, and he said to himself, "Oh, that mother's love is the prettiest thing I have seen on earth; I will carry that, too."

He winged his way back to heaven, but just outside the pearly gates he decided to examine his mementos to see how well they had made the trip. The flowers had withered, the baby's smile had faded, but the mother's love was still there in all its warmth and beauty. He discarded the withered flowers and the faded smile, gathered all the hosts of heaven around him, and said, "Here's the only thing I found on earth that would keep its beauty all the way to heaven—it is a mother's love."

I like that story because it symbolizes so much of what being a mom has been like for me. The roses and the baby's smile remind me of a little poem I once heard that talks about "Saying It with Flowers":

> A rose can say I love you,
> Orchids can enthrall.
> But a weed bouquet in a chubby fist—
> Oh my, that says it all!

Those chubby fists full of weeds and shy little smiles gave me some great Mother's Days, but later the bouquets and smiles faded. My love for my family had to absorb unbelievable pain and sorrow. Four tragedies hit us within a period of nine years, and any one of them could have been enough to sink the "Unsinkable Molly Brown."

"Your Husband Will Be a Vegetable"

The first blow came in 1966 when Bill and I were to be counselors for our church's young people's group at a conference grounds in the San Gabriel Mountains. Bill went on ahead that night, taking up supplies, and I planned to follow in my car after picking up a few last-minute items. Our two older boys, Steve and Tim, were going to the camp on the bus with their youth group, while Larry and Barney, our two younger boys, rode with me. So off we went on our great adventure.

The dark mountain road hadn't been used during the winter months, but it had been opened specifically for our church group to caravan up for a pre-Easter retreat. About ten miles from the conference grounds, I came upon a man sprawled in the middle of the road, covered with blood and glass. The only way I could tell it was Bill was by his clothes. I knew other cars would be coming along soon after me, so I left one of the children to stay with Bill in the road while I drove ten miles farther to camp to get to a telephone and call an ambulance.

It took almost two hours to get Bill to a hospital, but somehow he lived despite head injuries that left part of his brain exposed. Apparently Bill's car had hit some debris in the road and flipped over.

The events of the next couple of days are blurred for me, but I do remember a neurosurgeon and ophthalmologist calling me to their office to explain Bill's condition. The cranial nerves had been damaged, his vision was gone, and he was having seizures called "traumatic epilepsy." It was their opinion that he would never be able to function again within the family unit because he would be like a vegetable—without vision and without memory.

I couldn't believe it. Two days before we had been a happy family with four nice sons and no problems that I knew of. Now I was suddenly responsible for caring for four boys— two teen-agers and two under twelve.

When Bill was released from our local hospital, he couldn't see and didn't respond to any of us. In fact, he hardly moved, and it seemed the doctors had been right—he would be like a vegetable.

I knew I had to initiate getting some financial help, so I called in a friend to come and stay with Bill while I went out to get us on any available programs. First, I went to the office of Aid for the Blind; they gave Bill a free white cane. That was a start. Then I began seeking help in earnest from the Veterans Administration because Bill had been a lieutenant commander in the navy and would be eligible for benefits. I was told that he would have to be examined by their medical staff to determine his level of disability.

A few days later, I brought Bill in with me. When the Veterans Administration medical committee examined him and his medical records, they agreed with the other doctors that he could never function normally again. They told me that as soon as a bed opened up in the Sawtelle Veterans Hospital, he would be qualified to live there. I didn't tell them that that wasn't what I had in mind at all.

Next I contacted the Social Security office to initiate disability payments for Bill, as well as aid for our four boys and myself. After making more visits to the Veterans Administration and Social Security to finalize payments, I also filed insurance claims because Bill had been ruled as permanently disabled. Because we had a CalVet loan, the mortgage on the house was completely taken care of. And our life insurance policy, which had a clause covering bodily injury, paid Bill $20,000 for his loss of vision—$10,000 for each eye. As far as the insurance company was concerned, Bill would be blind for life, and he was due the full amount.

All this took time and energy. It was a challenge just learning how to get on or collect from these agencies. Just as I finished obtaining help from the Veterans Administration, Social Security Disability, Aid to the Blind, and our insurance policies . . . GOD HEALED HIM! It wasn't an immediate healing, but during all those months while I was out trying to find financial help, Bill slowly regained his strength, and his sight miraculously returned, as well as his mental faculties. One of the first signs that something good was happening was that Bill started asking me questions like, "Who are you? Do you work here?"

Bill's recovery was so complete that he started to consider going back to work. Here I had all these lovely checks flowing in regularly, and now I had to figure out a way to GET OFF all these programs! There were moments when I wondered why God couldn't have healed Bill *before I* had done all that work. If you think it's hard getting ON these programs, you should try getting OFF them! You don't just call the Veterans Administration and say, "Hello, remember my husband—the one you ruled as unrehabilitatable? Well, he is no longer blind, his brain damage is gone, he is suffering no more seizures, and he is going back to work as an engineer."

The Veterans Administration told me to bring Bill back to their offices, and their doctors would decide whether or not he was to be taken off disability. Our doctor went with us, and when Bill was examined by Veterans Administration doctors, they could hardly believe he was the same patient they had declared unrehabilitatable just a year before. Our doctor, a vibrant Christian man, tried to explain that Bill's restoration had been God's touch on his life, something not easily understood by those who have not experienced God's healing hand.

One agency that didn't give Bill clearance was the Department of Motor Vehicles. It seems they take a dim view of giving you back your driver's license when you've been blind and had brain damage, seizures, and the like. When Bill went back to work, I had to drive him both ways every day because no one at the DMV wanted to give him a road test so he could get a driver's license.

Bill wasn't able to get his driver's license reinstated for many months and, while driving him was a chore, our lives were beginning to seem more normal. We felt that God is the One who specializes in taking broken bodies and fractured minds and putting them back together again. The word *restore* means "to pop back into place," and God had, indeed, brought restoration in those two years since the accident in 1966.

And Then Steve Marched Off to Vietnam

While Bill was mending, the Vietnam War shifted into high gear and our second son, Steve, who was seventeen at the time and a senior in high school, got restless. Many of his buddies had already joined the marines, and he wanted to follow them. He disliked studying, and school was a pain to him. With reluctance, I signed the papers that allowed him to enter the U.S. Marines just a few months before his eighteenth birthday. Steve was a Christian, and that was my comfort as he went off to training. When he enlisted, we thought the Vietnam thing was winding down, but by the time he finished basic training, it was full-blown again, and he told us he would be shipped to Vietnam in March 1968.

I remember driving alone with Steve to Camp Pendleton the day he left. It was St. Patrick's Day, and we stopped for lunch at a place that was all decorated for the holiday. Normally, I would have enjoyed all the frivolity, but I was quiet and without much laughter.

We were early in arriving, so we had time to drive up a steep road that leads to a fabulous church in San Clemente, near Camp Pendleton. It has a spectacular view of the ocean, and although it was a dismal day with low clouds and fog, I have some indelible memories of our standing there by the church, looking out at the thrashing ocean below the cliffs. We prayed together there by the church, and then we slowly made the final lap of our trip to the marine base.

In my mind, I have a memory video of Steve swinging his green marine duffel bag over his shoulder . . . turning and waving . . . and then disappearing beyond the chain-link gates of Camp Pendleton.

His frequent letters from Vietnam reflected the spiritual growth that had surfaced in his life. When you are a Christian and your buddies are dropping all around you in battle, all you have left is your faith in God.

Although he was killed on July 28, 1968, it was not until three days later that a car marked "U.S. Marines" drove up to our home. Two young marines in full dress uniforms came to the door to tell us that Steve and his entire platoon had been wiped out in a battle near Da Nang.

When a loved one is in a dangerous situation, as Steve was, you live with constant apprehension and fear, but somehow, when it finally happens, it is like a "lifting"—that something is over. Indeed, life was over for Steve.

About ten days later, a call came from a mortuary near us, and a man's voice said, "Mrs. Johnson, you'll have to come up here and identify Steven's body because whenever a person dies in a foreign country, the law says that the body has to be identified."

Because Bill wasn't even driving a car yet, I decided he should be spared this gruesome situation, and I went by myself to the mortuary on a 100-degree-plus day in August. I was ushered into a viewing room by a little man dressed in a dark suit, who stood waiting as I looked into the hermetically sealed box and tried to determine if the brown bloated face before me belonged to my son. He had lain face down in a rice paddy for two days before being found. All they showed was the top half—I couldn't even be sure there was anything left of him below the belt. The little man kept standing there, and finally I decided that it must be Steve. I signed the paper that said, in effect, "This boy belongs to this box."

As I walked out of that mortuary, I thought, *By now we've surely had the cup of suffering. Bill is back to normal—well, almost. He still watches old John Wayne movies over and over and doesn't think he has seen them before, and he forgets birthdays and anniversaries . . . but I guess lots of men do that . . . and now we've lost this beautiful son who is our deposit in heaven.*

Steven's memorial service included the congregation singing "Safe in the Arms of Jesus," which was the song our church sang when he left to go to Vietnam. We had a little brochure printed with Steve's picture on the front, the message from his memorial service inside, and the plan of salvation on the back. And we began to share with other families who had lost sons in Vietnam. It was possible to obtain names from the *Los Angeles Times*, which printed a list each day of young men killed in action in Vietnam. We sent Steve's brochure to these families, feeling it was an opportunity to share our conviction that, as Christians, we have an endless hope because we know Jesus Christ.

Tim Called from the Yukon—Collect

The next five years went by quickly. The war in Vietnam finally ended, and we began to have closure in our healing from the loss of Steven.

Tim, our oldest son, was twenty-three. He had finished college and then graduated from the Los Angeles Police Academy in June 1973. He and his friend Ron had decided to take an extended vacation, so they drove to Alaska, where they planned to stay a few weeks, make a little money doing some temporary summer work, and then return home in early August to get ready to carry out their fall schedules.

I must tell you that, although Tim was a handsome and darling young man, he wasn't what I would call a lot of fun. That he worked during college at Rose Hills Mortuary tells you an awful lot. His idea of fun—and this was the epitome of fun for Tim—was to bring home the bows from mortuary bouquets and decorate our two dogs and cat with them. These bows had messages like, "May he rest in peace," or "God bless Grandpa Hiram." Whenever I came home and found the family pets all decked out in funeral ribbons, I knew Tim was "having fun" again.

After Tim arrived in Alaska, he wrote about his new friends and also mentioned that he had been baptized. This sort of hurt my feelings because he had already been baptized in our church, and I thought we had good water there, but I sensed some new spiritual dimensions in Tim's letters, unlike the boy we had known at home.

On August 1, 1973, I got a collect call from Tim. Now, I have always enjoyed having a new month. I change the sheets, take a bath, have my hair done, and we do something special to have FUN on the first of every new month. Of course, I do this at other times, too, but I always make the first of the month a special celebration.

Tim's first question was, "What are you doing, Mom, to celebrate the first of the month today?"

My quick response was, "Well, I was just HOPING for a collect call from you."

Tim went on to say, "Ron and I are on the way home. We should be there in about five days, and I can't wait to tell you what the Lord has done in my life. I've got a sparkle in my eye and a spring in my step, and I know the Lord is going to use my story all over."

I couldn't help but notice that Tim had an air of excitement in his voice; it sounded different from the conservative, well-modulated tone that was so familiar to me—one that seldom had shown much enthusiasm about anything. How exciting to think he would be home in five days to share with us all that had happened to change a quiet, sedate young man of twenty-three into an exciting, turned-on Christian.

Tim's call came around noon, and after we hung up, I started thinking of all of my efforts to get him entrenched in Christian activities. Once I had even bribed him with a new set of tires to get him to go to a Campus Crusade conference. But no matter what we did, Tim never took notes or seemed to act interested. He would just go with the flow, but would never get turned-on or excited . . . until NOW!

That night at dinner I was telling Bill and the other two boys, Larry and Barney, about Tim's phone call a few hours earlier. We were all laughing and enjoying what Tim had said, when the telephone rang. It was an officer of the Royal Canadian Mounted Police calling from White Horse, Yukon. It was hard to hear everything he was saying, but as the words came over the static-filled line, they came out like this: DRUNK BOYS IN A THREE-TON TRUCK . . . CROSSED THE CENTER LINE . . . HIT TIM'S LITTLE VOLKSWAGEN HEAD ON . . . TIM AND HIS FRIEND RON WERE KILLED . . . INSTRUCTIONS NEEDED FROM YOU AS TO HOW YOU WANT BURIAL PLANS MADE.

Tim and Ron had been immediately ushered into the presence of God! Stunned, I thought, *But this can't BE! I was just talking to him a few hours ago, and he was on the way home to share his story with us. He was to be home in five days! This can't be! I already have ONE deposit in heaven. I don't need TWO! Tim is our firstborn, a special gift. It just isn't FAIR!*

I lashed out at how this could happen to us . . . *again!*
Hadn't we had enough? How could God let this happen when
Tim was so thrilled about coming home to tell us of his excit-
ing spiritual experience?

A few hours later, we got a call from the pastor of the
church in Alaska where Tim had been attending during the
summer. He said, "We're not going to let those boys' story die
in the Yukon. We want to bring some folks down to share
what really happened in their lives."

I thanked him and told him I would let him know the date
of Tim's memorial service. Grief-stricken as I was, his offer to
share with us was comforting. Later at the memorial service
he told what had changed this dull, conservative boy into a
sparkling, shining personality so turned-on to spiritual
things. Tim had rededicated his life to the Lord, and his friend
Ron had become a Christian.

Our local newspaper published the story about the accident,
including pictures with the heading: "TWO BOYS KILLED BY
DRUNK DRIVER ON THE ALASKA HIGHWAY." The very
next day some darling young girls dropped by to tell us how
shocked they were to read of the accident. They brought along
letters Tim had written to them, which they had just received.
Evidently, the day before he had started for home, Tim had
written to several girls he used to go with, as well as some other
friends, and told them of his spiritual experience. His letter to
one girl said, "Please forgive me for being such a creep. . . ."
Any mother would wonder what that meant. Apparently, Tim
wasn't as boring as I thought he was!

Another Call from the Mortuary

It took over a week to get Tim's body shipped down from
the Yukon, and as we were preparing to have a memorial service, I received a phone call from the very same mortuary that
had called five years before to the very day. The man's voice
said, "Mrs. Johnson, I've never had to do this before, that is,
call the same family twice, but you'll have to come up here and
identify Tim's body since he was killed in a foreign country."

As I put down the phone, I remembered that Tim had been killed in the Yukon. Where was the Yukon, anyway? I had heard about Sergeant Preston and his sled dogs in the Yukon, but where actually was it? I looked at a map and saw that the Yukon is one of the territories that belong to Canada and that, indeed, it was part of a foreign country.

I had made this trip to the mortuary five years before and thought then it would be a once-in-a-lifetime ordeal. Now I was driving there again on a hot day in August to identify another boy in another box. As I stood there in the same viewing room, jumbled thoughts raced through my mind: *This is the same dumb carpeting they had five years ago, and the same dumb wallpaper, and I am standing here next to this same little man in the dark suit, looking at ANOTHER boy in a box. I can't BELIEVE this is happening all over again!*

It all seemed the same and so familiar, as if it had happened to me in another life, or in a dream! I wondered if my whole life would involve coming to this same mortuary every five years to look at boys in boxes. When you have been hit by a truck while sitting in the front seat of a Volkswagen, there isn't a whole lot left. You look at what they show you in the plain pine box, and then you sign another little paper saying this boy is your son Tim. But in no way does he look like the son you have had for twenty-three years.

Walking out of the mortuary that day, I could smell the fresh-cut grass and hear the crows cawing in the trees nearby. Suddenly I looked up, and in the blue sky was an image of Tim's smiling face. All around him it was bright gold and white, and he was saying to me, "Don't cry, Mom, because I'm not there. I am rejoicing around the throne of God."

It was as if God had wrapped me in his special comfort blanket of love that day. I've never had anything like that happen to me before or since, but I think God knew I needed that special sparkle just then to remind me that He still loves me, that I am His child, and that He never leaves us in the midst of our pain.

We had the memorial service for the boys, and many of

Tim's classmates from the Police Academy came and responded to the gospel message. Ron's parents had also accepted the Lord earlier that week. Later, articles about Tim and Ron appeared in several Christian magazines. The heading of a story in *Christian Life* said, "THEIR DEATH WAS ONLY A BEGINNING."

We began to see that, although they never made it home to share personally, Tim had been right: God was using their story all over the world to bring others to Him.

Barb, You're a Pro at This

A local pastor visited us a few days after Tim's memorial service. He knew about our previous loss with Steve and came to bring some words of comfort. His opening remark when I greeted him at the door was: "I'm not a bit worried about you, Barb, because you're a pro at this!"

A pro at what? A pro at losing another child? He probably meant that my inner strength would come from the Lord and I would get through it, but what he said came out uncaring and unhelpful, so lacking in understanding.

In some ways, losing Tim was more difficult than losing Steve. We had some time to prepare ourselves for Steve's passing. We knew for many months he was in a danger zone and the shadow of death was always on all of us. When it happened, it was a terrific shock, but still somewhat of a relief because the terrible apprehension was over.

In many ways, Steve's death was like having a loved one die after a long time of suffering with something like cancer or AIDS. Then you have some measure of time to prepare for it, and you have already dumped part of your cup of grief during those months. By the time of the actual death, it is like a lifting from the time of suffering, and you can begin to have closure.

But in Tim's case, there was no warning of impending disaster, no signal of distress. It was only his bright, happy voice saying he would be home in five days and then, WHACK! It was all over! One moment we were anticipating his arrival with excitement, and the next we learned he was in the presence of God. It had happened so quickly that there had been no preparation, not even a thought that his life would be snuffed out.

We had many wonderful Christian friends who came to visit us and tried to be comforting. They said things like, "Isn't it wonderful that Tim is with the Lord?" Well, yes, it was wonderful, but I wanted him HOME WITH US!

Or they would say, "How good it is that you have two other children left," and I would nod that, yes, that was good, but I wanted TIM! I would agree on the surface with people who were quoting Scriptures to me and wanting to make themselves feel better by having me zip up my anger and distress quickly. Inside, however, I wanted to escape from all of them and their nice little platitudes. I wanted to open—to lance— the big abscess inside me. I knew the verses they were quoting, and I believed them, but the raw edges of my heart were still bleeding too much. I needed to grieve.

To escape some of my "Ivory soap" Christian friends, I would drive alone at night to a dump a few miles away. I would park there and just sob, and sometimes even scream, to let out my pain. I would tell God how angry I was with these people for telling me how glad I should be that Tim was in heaven. I also told God how angry I was at Him for taking one so special and precious to me. This was my way of venting emotions that HAD to be released. God doesn't say not to grieve; instead, His Word says, ". . . that you may not grieve as others do who have no hope" (1 Thessalonians 4:13, RSV).

Looking back, I can see how Romans 8:28 and other verses that were quoted to me *are* all true. God is faithful, but the timing of these reminders was all wrong. Nice little plastic spiritual phrases don't help people unlock their grief. It is better to just put your arm around a grieving person and say, "I love you—and God loves you." Beyond that, it might be best to just shove a sock in your mouth and keep quiet. Don't try to reason with people in grief to persuade them to accept their loss. When a believer dies, it IS wonderful to know that person is with God, but at the moment when those who are left behind are bruised and bleeding, the simple truth is this:

> WHEN GRIEF IS THE FRESHEST,
> WORDS SHOULD BE THE FEWEST.

For a couple of weeks, I went to the dump nightly to rid myself of my grief. In recent years, the dump has been closed at night because so many people were getting mugged, but I believe God protected me when I was making my trips. By going there to grieve, I was able to come back to face my Christian friends who were spouting little spiritual platitudes that didn't work for me.

How to Dump Your Cup of Grief

Recently I met a lady who sells clothing in a department store. She told me that she had experienced the loss of a child and she couldn't work or wait on people because the tears kept coming all the time. She was a Christian and yet she hadn't been able to stop grieving. I shared with her a little plan that could help her "accelerate" her emotions:

"Get some sad music tapes, the saddest you can find," I told her. "Make sure everyone is out of the house, then go to the bedroom, unplug the phone, turn on the sad music, flop on the bed and just SOB.

"Set a timer for thirty minutes and during that time cry and pound the pillow. Let out your feelings—VENTILATE. If you're angry at God, that's okay. He won't say, 'Off to hell with YOU.' He still loves you.

"But get those deep hurts out through the avenue of tears. Do that every day for thirty days, and every day set your timer for one minute less. By the time thirty days have passed, you will have DUMPED a lot of your cup of grief."

Not long after I talked to her, the lady called me and said she had been taking my advice for only a week, and already she felt a lot better. She was to the point to where she could get through a whole day without the tears coming continually.

If you are experiencing difficulty in breaking open that deep abscess you have inside, perhaps this simple plan may help shorten your time of grief. There is no set amount of time to grieve that is considered proper or spiritual. But whatever time you need, "accelerating your emotions" may help you drain some of that pain and begin the road to recovery. The important thing is to have a closure time on your pain. Keep Psalm 84:5–7 ever in mind:

> Happy are those who are strong in the Lord, who want above all else to follow your steps. When they walk through the Valley of Weeping it will become a place of springs where pools of blessing and refreshment collect after rains! They will grow constantly in strength and each of them is invited to meet with the Lord in Zion. (TLB)

After Tim's memorial service in August, what helped me through the next few months was my continuing to try to help other people who had lost children. Now our ministry expanded beyond parents of Vietnam casualties, and we started talking with mothers and fathers who had lost their children in auto accidents or in other ways. I began speaking to parents' groups, telling them that the pain of losing two sons is incredible, but God's comfort blanket of love is still sufficient. I even got to the place where I could say that I was grateful for *two deposits in heaven*. We had been through dark times, and we had survived! What I didn't know was that total blackness was yet ahead of us.

🌸 Extra Thoughts to Take Along 🌸

Making the decision to have a child is momentous—it is to decide forever to have your heart go walking around outside your body.

— Elizabeth Stone, *Village Voice*

* * * *

THE WORLD'S GREATEST NEED

A little more kindness and a little less greed;
A little more giving and a little less need;
A little more smile and a little less frown;
A little less kicking a man when he's down;
A little more "we" and a little less "I";
A little more laughs and a little less cry;
A little more flowers on the pathway of life;
And fewer on graves at the end of the strife.

— C. Austin Miles
"A Little More and Less"[1]

* * * *

You *tolerate* my *trivia,*
laugh at my *lunacy*
and *care* when I *cry.*
That's what I call *TLC.*

— Source Unknown

* * * *

MORNING WILL COME

Brokenhearted . . .
How can I bear the pain?
So many plans . . . permanently interrupted.
So many dreams . . . shattered.
Hopes . . . dashed.
All gone.

Why? Why this?
Why us? Why me?
Helplessness . . . hopelessness . . .
Life will never be the same again.
Is it even worth living?
Where are you, God?

I'm right here beside you, my child.
Even though you may not feel my presence,
I'm holding you close under the shadow of my wings.
I will walk with you through this dark night.

Do not shrink from weeping.
I gave you tears for emotional release.
Don't try to hide your grief.
Let it become for you a source of healing,
A process of restoration,
For I have planned it so.
Those who mourn shall be blessed.
I'll be holding on to you,
Even when you feel you can't hold on to me.

Seek my face, child of mine.
Receive my promise, impossible as it may seem now,
That joy will come in the morning.
It may take much time,
But I will heal your broken heart.
I know the night seems endless,
But MORNING WILL COME.
I have promised.

— From the *Haven of Rest*
Newsletter

* * * *

*HELP ME TO REMEMBER, LORD, THAT
NOTHING WILL HAPPEN TODAY THAT
YOU AND I CAN'T HANDLE TOGETHER.*

— Source Unknown

* * * *

A SOFT PILLOW FOR TIRED HEARTS

*And we know that in all things God works for the good of those
who love him, who have been called according to his purpose.*

— Romans 8:28, NIV

3

It's Always Darkest
Just Before It Goes Totally Black

*EXPERIENCE is what you get
when you didn't get
what you wanted.*

"Why me . . . why did this happen to me?"

Has anyone gotten all the way through life without asking that question at least once or twice? (For some of us, maybe twice a day!)

"Why me? Why us? Why did two young boys get taken from our family?" I asked all those questions quietly in my heart for the next two years, even as I continued going out to speak and share comfort and hope with other parents. I wanted to believe that life would get better from here on. After all, we had two sons left—Larry, twenty, and Barney, seventeen. We had much to be thankful for.

"God Has His Hand on This Boy . . ."

Larry graduated from a local two-year junior college on Friday, June 13, 1975, and it was one of the proudest nights of my life. Larry had been president of his class and president of the school choir. He had been voted the most outstanding student and had offers of several scholarships. He had also just returned from Russia, where he traveled with a Christian singing group.

The pastor of one of the leading churches in Southern

California was the commencement speaker that night, and he also presented Larry with the Outstanding Student Award. To close the ceremonies, which were held outdoors in the college stadium, Larry led the entire audience in singing "The Battle Hymn of the Republic."

The commencement speaker talked with us afterward and commented on all of Larry's honors by saying, "I hope you have a car with a big trunk to carry home all this glory!" I said that all we had was a Chevy, and we all laughed. Then the speaker added, "I've spoken with your son, and I know that God has His hand on this boy and will use him in a wonderful way."

Bill and I were absolutely thrilled with his words about Larry. We took all the ribbons, cups, and awards home to display on our mantel. How proud we were of Larry and of his accomplishments!

The next day I planned to pick up my sister and her husband, who had been in Hawaii and were going to stop in our area for just twenty-four hours en route home to Minnesota. We wanted to make it a special event since it was the first time we had seen them since Tim's death.

We had it all arranged. I would pick them up at the L.A. airport, take them to Anaheim where we would all be staying at a motel near Disneyland, and then we would all go to the big bicentennial celebration at Disneyland that evening and enjoy the first presentation of the "Main Street Electrical Parade." Then we would stay in Anaheim, have some time together on Sunday, which was also Father's Day, and eat dinner at Knott's Berry Farm before they had to catch their plane.

Everything was in order for a fantastic time. What I didn't know was that this would be the most devastating day of my life!

As I headed out the door for the airport, someone telephoned, wanting to borrow Larry's big red Basic Youth Conflicts notebook. I went to his room and, as I lifted it out of his drawer, I saw a stack of homosexual magazines, pictures, and other stuff that I knew nothing about. There were also cassette tapes and letters from other young men. Why would

Larry HAVE this? Could it be a research project at school? No, school was all over now.

I began to shake inside, but I told myself, "You have to get to the airport . . . you can't fall apart right now. There must be some logical answer as to WHY he has this stuff in his drawer."

I didn't have time to think, or question, and I couldn't collapse—at least not right now. How could we have a homosexual child? I didn't know anyone who had one, I didn't want one, and surely this could not be! Bill and I had a ministry going to help hurting parents, but not THIS kind of hurt! It would be easier to kill him and kill myself rather than face this!

I quickly grabbed two arm loads of the "stuff" and threw it in the trunk of my car. I couldn't bear to have it in my home. Last night my car trunk had been full of glory, and now it was full of garbage! I hastily wrote a note to Larry, telling him to meet us as planned at the Disneyland flagpole at 8:00 P.M. that evening. Then I added that I had found the "stuff" and that I had it with me, just in case he might be looking for it.

My hands were shaking, my heart was pounding, and suddenly I felt as if I had an elephant on my chest. In the note I also told Larry that I loved him and God loved him and that if he would PLEASE help me get through the weekend with these relatives, then we would fix it on Monday! I had always believed that God and mothers can fix anything.

Driving to the airport, I began to feel all the symptoms of panic—shortness of breath, heaving inside, and throbbing in my head. It felt as if someone had shoved a shag rug down my throat and I was gagging on it. My eyes were so full of tears I could hardly see to drive. Then my teeth seemed to start to itch! Evidently the nerve endings around my mouth were responding to the stress, but I just HAD to hold together until the relatives left the next day.

I got to the airport just in time to meet Janet and Mel as they came off the plane. Her first words were, "Boy, you look terrible. Are you sick?"

I said, "Of course not; it was just something I couldn't swallow." (Couldn't swallow was right!)

They had already been to baggage claim, and I saw that Janet had two pieces of purple luggage. Now, I knew nothing about homosexuality and even less about lesbianism, but I had heard somewhere that lesbians like purple. A crazy thought hit me: *MY SISTER IS A LESBIAN! SHE HAS PUR-PLE LUGGAGE! She works for the Billy Graham Evangelistic Association, is married to a minister, and she has PURPLE luggage! My own sister must be a lesbian because of this purple luggage!*

I Didn't Dare Open the Trunk!

When we got to my car, I became frantic trying to think of how I could avoid opening my car trunk. All of Larry's homosexual "stuff" was in there, and I had not bothered to cover it up with a blanket. Mel and Janet had brought some pine-apples from Hawaii, as well as some of those dreadful leis that smell like funerals, and somehow I scrunched them and their belongings in the backseat without opening the trunk. We started for Anaheim and the motel, and I prayed I could ignore my panic symptoms and somehow stay on the road.

My mind was so shattered from finding out about Larry that it seemed as if the whole world were crashing around me. If my own son, whom I had loved and raised for twenty years, was a homosexual and my sister was a lesbian, what was left to believe in? I had heard of people who live in "la-la land," and I was definitely on the way there myself. I felt as if I had been on another planet and had just come back to visit the world. I wanted to go back to where I had come from, but there was no place to escape the weirdness of it all.

As we drove along the freeway, the crazy thoughts would not leave my tortured mind. My brother-in-law pointed out the big A on the Angels' Stadium, and all I could think of was, *Oh, they're all homosexuals, they're all homosexuals!* It seemed to me that the shades had gone up and everyone had become homosexual.

We got to the motel where Janet and Mel changed into more comfortable clothes, and then we crossed the street to Disneyland. It was a special weekend, with the bicentennial celebration, the first night of the Main Street Electrical Parade scheduled, and it was also Flag Day. Instead of the usual A-B-C-D-E coupon books Disneyland used for tickets, we were all given a red, white, and blue headband with a big feather sticking out of it. On the headband were the words "I'M A YANKEE DOODLE DANDY" in bold, bright letters. You couldn't escape wearing the headband because it was your ticket to the park that evening.

So there I was, trying to act normal in Disneyland with what seemed like fifty thousand people around me all wearing "I'M A YANKEE DOODLE DANDY" feathered headbands. And all the while I kept wondering if everyone I saw was a homosexual!

As 8:00 P.M. drew near, we went over to the flagpole, and Bill went off to buy popcorn. Bill is loving and dependable, but it seems that any time there is a crisis, he is off buying popcorn. I tell him that when he dies, I'm going to have inscribed on his tombstone, "Bill is not here, he's out buying popcorn."

Janet, Mel, and I greeted Larry as he walked up. The last time we had all been together was at Tim's funeral, so they were really glad to see him. I wasn't sure I was, but I knew I couldn't throw up or anything—not just yet.

Then Tinker Bell Flew across the Sky!

So we all stood there at the flagpole with a sea of Yankee Doodle humanity flowing by. Just then, one of Disneyland's special attractions came sailing across the sky. It was the Tinker Bell Fairy (suspended on a wire, of course) loudly hailing the Main Street Electrical Parade, scheduled to start in a few minutes. That only set my mind off again—the whole world was full of this homosexual stuff! Even the Tinker Bell Fairy!

Just then Janet said, "It's so crowded and hot here, I think Mel and I will go see Mr. Lincoln." The Mr. Lincoln display was only a few feet away, so I said, "Go ahead. Larry and I have seen it many times, so go ahead." I was desperate to have a few minutes to talk with Larry and implore him to help me get through the weekend until Mel and Janet left on the plane Sunday afternoon.

And now Larry and I were alone in front of the flagpole at Disneyland with fifty thousand people surrounding us. We were both wearing the little headbands with the feathers saying, "I'M A YANKEE DOODLE DANDY." And the first thing Larry said was, "I'm a homosexual, or maybe I'm a bi-sexual."

I didn't know what to say. A bi-sexual? The word *homosexual* was in the Bible, but *bi-sexual* I'd never heard—it sounded like sex twice a month. While I was trying to figure that out, a lady came by, pushing a stroller with her chubby child in it. The stroller rammed into my foot, and a sharp edge dug into my leg and it started to bleed.

I thought, *Oh, how merciful God is. I won't have to kill him tomorrow. I won't even have to kill myself because I'm going to bleed to death right here.* I kept thinking of 1 Corinthians 10:13: God had made a way of escape so that I could bear all this. I was just going to hemorrhage right here and die right in front of the "Lost Children" sign at the Disneyland flagpole with fifty thousand people going by, all wearing headbands announcing "I'M A YANKEE DOODLE DANDY."

How wonderful—it was almost euphoric! I wouldn't have to worry about killing myself or killing him, or doing anything, and nobody would ever know. But THEN I realized that my car trunk was still full of homosexual magazines, and I couldn't die now because my husband would find all that and think they were mine. About then, Larry said he didn't feel well, that he wanted to get out of there. I thought to myself, *You're sick . . . but I'm dying! Yes, why don't you just go home, and we'll fix it tomorrow. God and mothers can fix anything . . . can't they?*

Mel and Janet emerged out of the crowd and greeted Larry enthusiastically, but all Larry could say was that he didn't feel too good because he was tired after rehearsing all day with a Christian singing group! After a few moments of polite chitchat, he excused himself and left.

Just a minute or two later, Bill returned with his popcorn,

and my younger son, Barney, and his friend stopped by for a few minutes and then left because they were bored with the whole thing and wanted to head home to watch the motorcycle races on TV. (When you live as close to Disneyland as we do, it's no big deal.)

So Mel, Janet, Bill, and I wandered around Disneyland and I kept looking at everyone and thinking that the whole world was homosexual. I saw Mickey Mouse and Minnie Mouse, and I was sure they were homosexual, too. It was as if everyone had a big H stamped on his forehead.

"He Can't Be; He's a Christian"

We went back to the motel for the night, and while Bill slept, I wept, moaned, and groaned into a pillow. It felt as if a bull were goring me inside. About 4:30 A.M. on Sunday, which was Father's Day, my husband finally woke up saying, "What's the matter with you?"

I gasped, "I think I'm having a heart attack. I don't know what you call it, but I think I'm dying. I can't breathe, and I'm choking. It feels as if I've got a rug in my throat, and my teeth itch."

Bill said, "Well, I thought you were acting strange last night. I know something is wrong. What is it?"

"Well, I'm glad you noticed! Last night I just found out that Larry is a h-h-h-h-hooomoooo . . ." I could hardly say the words . . . "a homosexual."

Bill was aghast. "He CAN'T be; he's a Christian!"

"Well, that's what I thought. But he is. You should see what I have in my car trunk. Or maybe he's a bi-sexual; that's what he told me."

Hearing that Larry might be bi-sexual shocked Bill more than anything else. He bolted out of bed and started putting his clothes on. I said, "It's 4:30 in the morning; where are you going?"

"Why, I'm going HOME to fix him," said Bill, and he was gone.

So I lay there gasping and choking, wondering how I'd ever

get through this. My husband was driving twenty-five miles back to our house to "fix his kid," and I thought, *Well, I'll just be dead when he comes back. That's all, I'll just be dead; I just can't live through this. I'll be dead when he comes back.*

About then my sister, hearing the ruckus, knocked on our door, came in, and asked anxiously, "What's wrong? Why did Bill leave?"

All I could think of was, "He went home to shave." What else was I going to say? We had checked into a motel, paid good money, so where would my husband go at 4:30 in the morning?

"No, I know something is wrong. You had a fight with Bill, didn't you?"

If only she had been right—that would have been no problem at all! Instead, I had no choice; I would have to start Father's Day at 4:30 in the morning telling my sister that my son is a homosexual.

I stumbled out to my car and brought in a whole armload of the homosexual magazines and threw them on the bed. Then I said, *"Your nephew* [I couldn't say "my son"]) is a homosexual."

She sputtered, "He CAN'T be; he's a Christian."

There we stood, the daughters of a minister, both having led very sheltered lives while growing up. We stared at all the pictures of naked men and all the rest of that terrible stuff. We had never seen anything pornographic before. About the closest we had come to pornography was the men's underwear section of the Montgomery Ward's catalogue.

And as we stood there, frozen in shock, poring over all that garbage, in walked my brother-in-law, a very proper, godly man. He questioned what was going on because he could hear me sobbing and crying, and he thought perhaps Janet and I were having some sort of fight. And then he saw the pictures on the bed.

Janet explained, "This stuff belongs to Larry—he's a homosexual."

And Mel's instant response was, "Why, he CAN'T be; he's a Christian!"

When Bill came back, we were all still in the room, looking at the magazines in bewilderment with no idea what to say. All Bill offered was, "I talked to Larry. There's nothing really wrong with him. You're just too emotional about this. It's just a phase. All kids go through a phase, and this is just a phase."

Oh, I wanted to believe that, but I knew Bill was wrong. He didn't even know what a bi-sexual was, so how did he know what was really wrong with Larry? Later, we went to church and on to Father's Day dinner at Knott's Berry Farm. It is all a blur to me, but I finally got Mel and Janet to the plane, and they went back to Minneapolis, where I was sure nobody ever had homosexual problems.

Tears blinded me as I drove home alone from the airport. Bill had taken his car and driven over to give Father's Day presents to his dad, and when I got home I found Larry there. We stood in the living room toe to toe, and it quickly escalated into a full-scale confrontation. I was sobbing bitterly and spouting Bible verses. He began to cry, too, and our conversation went in vicious circles.

I was so hysterical I could hardly make sense. Larry was exploding with anger because he had been exposed. (Later on he told me he never would have told us if I hadn't found the stuff.) I begged him to sit down and tell me how all this could be! Instead, he said violent and vicious things to me in the heat of his anger and used words I had never heard before or since from him.

I couldn't bear his accusations and obscenities. Instantly my hand shot upward and I slapped Larry's face hard. He grabbed my shoulders and pushed me full force against a grandfather clock. This was unbelievable! I was having a physical confrontation with this darling son who was the light of our home for twenty years! After shoving me against the clock, he fled to his room and slammed the door.

I heard him sobbing in his room, but my anger, denial, and guilt all kept me from going in to comfort him. COMFORT HIM? When HE was destroying our family?

In my desperate effort to make him respond, I had uttered

threats and unloving things like, "I would rather have you be DEAD than be a homosexual!" At that moment I loved Larry, but I hated that part of him. I wanted to hug him, but I wanted to kill him—I was a kaleidoscope of emotional shock. It would be later that I learned that parents say all kinds of unreal things to their kids when they learn they are homosexual. In my own emotional frenzy, all I could do was quote Bible verses about homosexuality. And all the while I was also denying that this could really be happening to us.

Other parents have told me the same thing. When they learn of their child's homosexuality, they want to take them out of their will, take away the car, or do whatever they can do to control them. But that doesn't work. You just can't do it that way. This is something I had to learn. And it wasn't easy.

Devastating despair overwhelmed me, and I flung myself on my bed and sobbed for hours. Larry didn't come out of his room the rest of the day . . . no supper was fixed . . . I didn't answer the phone. I just lay there on my bed, hoping and praying that tomorrow I could find some answers. I would go to the Hot Line in Anaheim. Surely THEY would tell me how to fix this kid!

On Monday morning I went to a Hot Line organization that was supposed to offer help to homosexuals, but first I needed some help for *me*—someone to tell me I would get through this alive. I went in and blurted out, "I just found out that my son is a homosexual, and I want to talk to a mother who can help me."

And they said, "Well, we don't have any mothers, but we have two ex-homosexuals you can talk to."

Exasperated, I sputtered, "Forget it! I *have* one of those— that's why I'm here!"

I just turned around, stomped out, and slammed the door. I didn't want to talk to any kind of homosexual, ex- or other- wise. I wanted to talk to a mother who had been through what I was going through and who could tell me I wasn't going to die. As I got in the car, I thought, *Lord, if I ever get through this— if I don't die or end up in a home for the bewildered—I promise that*

I'll start some kind of group to help parents who have this kind of terrible thing happen to them. (We promise a lot when we think we're going to die anyway.)

And Then, a Final Zinger

When I got back home, one more shock awaited me. Larry's room was totally empty. I had been gone only an hour and a half, but in that time he had cleaned out everything and left. Out in the hall two little plaques hung side by side. One said, "TO THE MOST WONDERFUL FATHER OF THE YEAR." Larry had given that to Bill just the day before. The other one said, "TO THE MOST WONDERFUL MOTHER OF THE YEAR," and he'd given that to me just a month before on Mother's Day. Now he was gone, and all we had were the two plaques telling us how wonderful we were.

I called Bill at work and told him Larry was gone and that he'd taken the little Volkswagen that was registered to me; the insurance was also in my name. Bill said he was sure Larry would be back, but I wondered where he would go.

I didn't know what to do. Should I go down to the DMV and tell them that my kid had taken off with a Volkswagen registered to me? Should I cancel the insurance on the car? I just didn't know what to tell people, and I wasn't sure I would survive.

How I did survive is recorded in a daily log that I included in *Where Does a Mother Go to Resign?* During the next few months, I stayed home, languishing in my bedroom, counting the roses on the wallpaper. I couldn't stand seeing anyone, and even going to the grocery store brought waves of panic. If I saw cartons of milk labeled HOMOGENIZED, I would immediately think that even the milk had something homo-sexual in it.

As hard as losing Steve and then Tim was, at least I could count them as deposits in heaven. But now my third son had disappeared into the gay lifestyle, and I had no idea where he was or if I'd ever see him again.

And I couldn't tell any of my Christian friends what had

happened. I felt too guilty, and besides, how could most Christians understand something as unreal as this?

So I just hid away in my bedroom, not wanting to see anyone, doing no cooking or cleaning and very little eating. Bill put up some get-well cards on the mantel, so if anyone did come by, they might say, "Poor Barbara is still recovering from the loss of her two sons" and tend to ignore the disarray and clutter.

Bill just ate popcorn for most of that first year after Larry left. Fortunately, Barney, our younger son, worked at Taco Bell, so at least he had something to eat. Taco Bell wrappers started piling up all over the house along with the popcorn, which got spilled in strange places.

From the Pits to the Couch

Eventually, Bill insisted that I get help for my depression. I chose to see Dr. Wells, a psychologist who also happened to be a personal friend. On my first visit he shocked me by saying, "Don't blame yourself for this . . . we all have to make choices . . . it is a very black picture for you to accept. In my professional experience, I have had little success in changing the orientation of homosexuals. If and when Larry does contact you, don't talk to him about change."

"What do you mean, don't talk about change?" I sputtered. "Of course we're going to talk about change—we can't have THIS." I went on to berate Dr. Wells with Bible verses. How could he be a Christian and say God couldn't change Larry? I quoted him Scripture about how God changes *all things*, but Dr. Wells was unmoved as he patiently listened to my arguments. He seemed to understand I couldn't accept what he was telling me—at least at that time. After all, I wanted to fix Larry—as soon as possible.

To get some additional help, I began writing to top evangelical leaders around the country, asking for their counsel. In a few days I began getting their replies, which contained Scripture passages condemning homosexuality, prayer cloths, and bottles of oil. I even got one suggestion to send his shorts to a certain address where they would be prayed for and his demon cast out. I didn't know where Larry was, and I sure didn't know where his shorts were!

Almost weekly, Dr. Wells and I continued our dialogue. One day, after Larry had been gone eleven months, Dr. Wells told me, "Well, if Larry has been gone eleven months, very possibly he will never come home again. He has probably found his emotional support in the gay lifestyle."

This really put me on a downer, and I went into a zombie-like trance! Dr. Wells decided he'd better call Bill. I remember him saying, "She's in severe depression. We should commit her to a place where she can get twenty-four-hour professional care because she's exhibiting suicidal feelings."

Bill is Swedish and somewhat stingy. I suppose *frugal* would be a kinder word, but stingy is more accurate. Bill's answer was, "Well, if my insurance will cover her, she can go. But if it costs any money, I think she can stay home—she's not VICIOUS or anything."

And so those were my options. If Bill's insurance covered me, I could go make baskets at the home for the bewildered, and if it didn't pay, I could stay home and count the roses on the wallpaper.

Dr. Wells Was Right about Suicide

A day or two later as Bill was leaving for work, he told me that when he got home that night, he'd know if his insurance would cover me. After he left, I climbed into the car and started driving. I couldn't go on like this. I wasn't functioning as a wife or a mother. I wasn't anything.

I'm just like a zombie or a zero with the rim rubbed out—I'm nothing, I thought. *I just can't believe that God would let all this happen to me and still really love me.*

I knew about a big viaduct on Ball Road going to Disneyland, and I thought I would just drive the car right off that viaduct, be killed, and all my troubles would be over. But as I started up the viaduct, I got to thinking, *What if I'm just maimed, and then I'll be crippled and making baskets for the rest of my life?*

By the time I got to the top of the viaduct, I was sure I didn't want to kill myself, and then I said, "I can't believe it, Lord, but I've gotten to this point where I actually want to drive my car off a viaduct and kill myself. I'm taking out a hammer in my imagination, and I'm going to nail that kid to the Cross because I can't handle this anymore. I'm tired of this elephant on my chest, my teeth itching, and this rug in my throat. This has been going on for eleven months, and I thought I gave it all to You long ago. But this time I'm saying that I'm really nailing him to the Cross, I'm giving him to You, and if he never comes home and I never see him again, *whatever, Lord. Whatever happens,* I'm nailing that kid to the Cross and giving him to YOU!"

"Whatever, Lord," Was the Key

When I said those words, "Whatever, Lord," it seemed to release a million little sparkles inside me. The shag rug came out of my throat, my teeth stopped itching, and the elephant got off my chest for the first time in eleven months. All I'd said was, "Whatever, Lord," instead of my usual, "Why *me?* Why *my* kid? Why is my life such a mess? Why me?" All the heaviness was GONE!

For me, saying, "Whatever, Lord," was like Job saying, "Though he slay me, yet will I trust in him" (Job 13:15, KJV). I turned that car around, and for the first time in eleven months I could take a deep breath. I sang all the way home—"The King Is Coming" and "Come On Down, Lord Jesus." I hadn't sung for eleven months, but that day I sang all the way home.

I called Bill, and I was so excited that I talked fast. So Bill had a hard time making sense of my flood of words.

"Where have you been?" he questioned.

"Well, I went down toward Disneyland, and I was going to kill myself by driving off the viaduct, but instead I said, 'Whatever, Lord,' and nailed him to the Cross.

"You *WHAT?*" Bill demanded.

"I nailed him to the Cross," and I'm sure Bill was thinking, I *should have put her in the home for the bewildered yesterday. I've waited too long.*

"Don't go anywhere. Stay there; I'm coming right home,"

and he hung up. I tried to tell him that he didn't have to come home, that I was fine, but he raced home anyway and sat me down for some answers. My babbling had him envisioning our kid nailed somehow on the 57 Freeway! Just a few years before, Bill had been the one with brain damage, but now he reasoned gently with me as if he were my father or a counselor. I went through the whole thing again, and finally he seemed to understand that I'd been able to let Larry go and give the whole problem to God.

Very relieved he said, "I just can't believe what's happened, but I'll tell you one thing. I'm glad you're better because my insurance didn't cover you anyway."

The Prodigal Returns—Temporarily

The next day I started cleaning the house—for the first time in eleven months. Can you imagine what it was like? Popcorn kernels and Taco Bell wrappers everywhere. I got out some giant trash bags, put on some Christian records, and as I was singing my way through the trash, the phone rang.

It was Larry.

"Mom, I'm at In-N-Out Hamburgers, and I want to bring you one. What do you want on it?"

If Larry had called the day before, I would have said, "You little creep! Don't you know they're ready to put me in the home for the bewildered?" But instead, I just said, "Oh, Honey, you come on home—anything is fine."

I knew that Larry was just testing the water to see if it was safe to come back. A little while later, in he walked, and we ate hamburgers together. Because he was nervous, I didn't ask him many questions, but I did find out he was going to school at UCLA and living alone. He had gotten along fine during the past eleven months, and I didn't press him for a lot more information than that.

We talked and shared for quite a while, and then he left. But he came back the next week to talk to Bill and his brother, Barney. He kept coming back weekends and seemed glad to be with us. Every time we saw him, we'd talk mostly about surface things. I didn't want to delve into anything about homosexuality—I just wanted our relationship to be restored.

Larry continued to stay in close contact by coming over on weekends and calling us often. The next year he was best man at Barney's wedding, and the following June he graduated with honors from UCLA. As glad as I was when he reconnected with the family, I still had a sense of doubt and foreboding. I walked on eggs, fearing that I'd say the wrong thing, cause a big explosion, and estrange him from us again.

But Larry wasn't the same kid anymore. He looked different, sounded different. We couldn't talk about anything spiritual. All we ever talked about were surface things. It seemed as if he had arrived from another planet, but I kept telling myself everything would be all right. I just wanted to put all the bad days behind us and not talk about it, but I eventually learned it wasn't behind us at all.

Early in 1979, a publisher contacted me and asked me if I would write my story. They didn't know much about Larry, but they knew what had happened to our two other boys.

I asked Larry, "How would you feel if I wrote all about this in a book?"

Larry said he didn't care, but I believe that he really didn't think I could do it anyway. I told the publisher I had never written anything, but one of the editors said, "Well, the Holy Spirit will propel it."

And that's exactly what happened. The book poured out of me in eight weeks, and I wrote about our experiences right up to the time Larry had come back home. It was published in the fall of 1979, and the reaction surprised everyone, especially me. I started getting phone calls, inquiries, and requests to be on radio and television. A major book distributor picked up *Where Does a Mother Go to Resign?* and it was soon on book racks in airports and supermarkets all over the country.

How SPATULA Got Started

I was thrilled with the response to *Where Does a Mother Go to Resign?* because it provided an excellent tool for SPATULA, the ministry for hurting parents we started in 1977. I had been volunteering at the Hot Line to give help to other parents, especially mothers, and I kept getting requests to begin some kind of support group that could meet weekly in my area. When some friends at the Hot Line asked me what I needed in order to work with parents, I replied that I needed about one hundred spatulas to scrape them off the ceiling. It was their suggestion that we call my parents' group SPATULA, since scraping them off the walls and ceilings was what I was doing.

The name stuck, and I began meeting every Thursday night with a group of women, each of whom was welcomed into the group officially by receiving a large, red, plastic spatula. Our goal at Spatula is to provide a cushion of intensive care for mothers who are on the ceiling after learning about their homosexual children or who have endured the death of a child. The first Spatula group was so successful, others sprang up in other major cities around the country and *Christian Life* magazine ran a story. I was thankful that God helped me keep the promise I'd made two years earlier when I stormed out of the Hot Line office that couldn't give me any help.

"I'm Going to Disown My Whole Family!"

While things were going well with Spatula, our relationship with Larry was deteriorating. After *Where Does a Mother Go to Resign?* came out, I didn't hear from him for a while. Then he came over to see me, angry and agitated. He brought along his Bible as well as his big red Basic Youth Conflicts notebook. He had always loved Basic Youth material and always said he believed it was the only way to live. That day he threw the Bible and the notebook down and said, "I don't want any part of this . . . you can have it all . . . it's not part of my life anymore . . . I'm doing my own thing!"

My response was total shock and disbelief. He walked out before I could even say much of anything to him. I didn't hear from him for several weeks, and then just after the New Year he called, sounding irate. He said, "How do you think I feel when I see that book at the airport and in Piggly Wiggly markets?

Everywhere I see that book. I turn on TV and there you are . . . I turn on the radio and you're even on the radio . . ."

I was surprised and reminded Larry, "Well, you said I could write it . . ."

"Yeah, I suppose I did. But I never thought you could do it—such a dreary story, and who would read it anyway?"

"Apparently lots of people are reading it and getting lots of help . . ."

"Well, I don't like it. I have a lover in my life now, and I'm going to change my name and disown the family. I never want to see any of you again."

I gasped when he used the word *lover*. He didn't say, "I'm living with somebody." He said emphatically, "I have a lover," and it just blew me away. The conversation got pretty tense after that, but somehow I kept myself together. I realized then that we had already lost him long ago. Nonetheless, all I could feel for him was love.

I recall saying, "Larry, homosexuality is not God's best for anybody, and I want God's best for you. I can't change your life, but there are two things I can do for you—love you and pray for you. And until they close the casket on my head and put a lily in my hand, I'm going to do just that. Just remember—we love you unconditionally, and the porch light is always on for you."

Larry was unmoved by my words, and he hung up in anger, letting me know that we definitely would not hear from him EVER again. Well, that wasn't quite true. We did hear from him again when an official form arrived in the mail saying that he had changed his name and had disowned us. Now my vow of "Whatever, Lord . . ." had come back to challenge me. Did I mean what I promised God back there on the viaduct on Ball Road three years ago, or didn't I?

The rest of this book comes out of the ideas and philosophies that came to mold my life as I spent over six long years never hearing from Larry. During those years, I learned the value of laughter, how to deal with guilt feelings, and how to stay calm when hysteria would well up within. Above all, I learned the meaning of hope. And it's hope I want to talk about next.

Extra Thoughts to Take Along

THE PORCH LIGHT

"The porch light's always on for you,"
She said that day he left.
"The porch light's always on." That's all.
And then the front door slammed.

The porch light burned through springtime nights.
And twinkled under summer stars.
It glowed on with the harvest moon.
And bounced off snowdrifts in the yard.

The porch light burned each night for years,
A symbol of the love
That waited just inside the door,
And waited on, and waited on.

In dreams, he saw it every night
But stayed outside its glow.
Still, knowing that it burned for him,
He'd think sometimes . . . but, no.
It happened unexpectedly.
He stumbled toward the Light
And that Light led to another—
On a porch—still on, still bright.

Inside a mother waited,
Heart still yearning, arms still open,
Love still ready to spill over.
Now rejoicing, "He's come home!"

"The porch light's always on for you,"
God said to us that day.
"The porch light's always on." It shines
From a cross on Calvary.

— Ann Luna

* * * *

WHEN LIFE GETS HARD

There comes a time in everyone's life when trouble and difficulties seem to gang up. When this happens—when life gets hard—what is the creative way to handle things?

FIRST: Don't try to do it all yourself. Do not struggle and fret. Do not strain and complain. Do all you can about things and then put everything into God's hands, trusting Him to bring it out right. You can depend upon God. He will not fail you. Let go and let God.

SECOND: Pray for guidance and believe that direction is *now* being given you. Believe this guidance can be trusted. Depend upon it, for it won't fail you.

THIRD: Pray for and practice a calm attitude. Disturbing things will remain disturbing as long as you are disturbed. But when you become peaceful, conditions will iron themselves out. You cannot think creatively when your mind is upset. Remember: upset minds upset; peaceful minds "peacefulize."

FOURTH: Saturate your consciousness with faith, the creative faith that things will turn out right. Say aloud every day several times: "Thou wilt keep him in perfect peace, whose mind is stayed on thee" (Isaiah 26:3, KJV). "In quietness and in confidence shall be your strength" (Isaiah 30:15, KJV). "Peace I give unto you: not as the world giveth, give I unto you. Let not your heart be troubled, neither let it be afraid" (John 14:27, KJV).

FIFTH: Remind yourself of one great truth: hard experiences *will* pass away. They will yield. They *can* be changed. So just hold on, with God's help.

SIXTH: There is always a light in the darkness. Believe that. Look for that light. The light is the love of God. "Thy word is a lamp unto my feet, and a light unto my path" (Psalm 119:105, KJV). Go ahead into the darkness unafraid.

SEVENTH: Ask the Lord to release your own creative ingenuity, your own strength and wisdom, which taken together can, for a fact, handle any problem successfully.

EIGHTH: Never forget that God cares for you, that He loves you. He wants to help you. Turn to Him, and gratefully accept His help.

NINTH: Remember that all human beings experience troubles similar to your own. Many years ago a graduating class gave a stone bench to their university on which were graven these words: "To those who sit here sorrowing or rejoicing: greetings. So also did we in our time."

TENTH: Finally, hold on to this great promise: "God is our refuge and strength, a very present help in trouble" (Psalm 46:1). And this is the truth. God will see you through, and a brighter day will dawn for you.

— Source Unknown

4

I Feel So Much Better Now That I've Given Up Hope*

Life is easier than you think—
All you have to do is:
Accept the impossible,
Do without the indispensable,
Bear the intolerable
and
Be able to smile at anything.

—Source Unknown

When we received that official notarized form saying Larry had disowned us and changed his name, I couldn't help but think of what the Bible says to Christians who are facing black times: "Consider it pure joy, my brothers, whenever you face trials of many kinds, because you know that the testing of your faith develops perseverance. Perseverance must finish its work so that you may be mature and complete, not lacking anything" (James 1:2–4, NIV).

The first time Larry left, I thought I had learned something about perseverance. Now that he was gone again—this time apparently for good—I saw that God still had some trials in mind to help me grow and mature. Growing is a lifetime job, and we grow most when we're down in the valley, where the fertilizer is.

---

*For the title of this chapter I am indebted to Ashleigh Brilliant, Pot-Shots No. 519, © Brilliant Enterprises 1974. Used by permission.

While I was talking with a friend, she got a telephone call bringing some disturbing news. Instead of panic, her response was, "Well, here we GROW again!" She was right. We can go through painful trials, or we can *grow* through them.

One of the best descriptions I've ever heard of how it feels to experience an ongoing trial came from a lady who was feeling desperate and undone. There just was no light in sight at the end of her tunnel. She told me, "I feel like I've been living in a parenthesis since I learned about my son. I keep trying to move the parenthesis, and it keeps stretching out, and I am *still* in this horrible parenthesis in my life!"

My Parenthesis Had Never Ended

Fortunately, when Larry left that second time, I was better prepared for my parenthesis—a time of trial and struggle that can be brief or seemingly endless. Actually, Larry's bitter reaction to *Where Does a Mother Go to Resign?* wasn't a new parenthesis at all. His angry exit from our lives only forced me to realize that the problem that began for me on that night at the flagpole on Disneyland's Main Street had really never gone away. The story was just continuing with a new chapter.

When Larry returned after his first absence of eleven months, I thought everything was "okay," and so did Bill. Larry's "phase" was over, and we just didn't talk about it. How wrong we were.

But now here I was, locked in another measurement of time and, until God chose to remove the ends of the parenthesis, I would have to live in another vacuum. Some people might call it a pit or a cave, but whatever you choose to call it, it's a contained situation. You can't go back and wish it were only a day ago or even two years ago. And you can't jump ahead—out of the pit into a happy, carefree time. Until God kicks the ends out of your parenthesis, you have to handle today, today.

This doesn't mean you ignore or negate God's promises and instructions. But you may have to settle for not being sure you understand what's going on—at least at the moment.

I love the cartoon caption that says, "Mother said there'd be days like this . . . she failed to mention that they could go on for months at a time."

One thing that helps is not to deny you're in the process. If you hurt, admit it. As one "bumper snicker" advises:

> WHEN YOU'RE DOWN AND OUT
> LIFT UP YOUR HEAD AND SHOUT . . .
> "I'M DOWN AND OUT!"

That's the first step in handling your parenthesis. The next step is to realize that whatever the problem is, *it won't last forever*. I was talking to a gal who has some real problems, and she told me her favorite Scripture verse is, "And it came to pass . . ." I looked at her rather quizzically and she laughed and added, "Just think, all this could have come to STAY!"

Pain Has a "Passing Through" Stage

Since every parenthesis has come to pass, you have to go through a "passing through" stage. It's okay to admit you're suffering and hurting, and you might even be angry with God. But then you go on to make the most of this particular time frame. As the passage from James reminds us, it's a chance to grow. So give it all you've got, and see what you can learn from this pain.

All the promises of God are there, and they're real, and they're true, but right now you're bleeding, you're raw and hurting, and you have to hang on to those promises even if they don't seem to work for you at the moment. As you go through the pain, it will lessen. The pain will flatten out and dilute itself, and then you can look back and realize how far you've come. You can start living with the parenthesis behind you! There may be occasional dips back into the pits, but you know you are getting out of that parenthetical period.

Every time you feel closed in, or like you are smothering in a tight little box with the lid nailed down, imagine you are stepping over that horrid little parenthesis. You *are* going to get over this, and when you do climb over it and then look back you will realize you've reached new gains and new values. You have completed a segment of growth as a person.

If any of God's prophets knew what it was like to go through a parenthesis, it had to be Jeremiah. In fact, you could say his entire life was one parenthesis after the other. And yet God told him, "For I know the plans I have for you. . . . They are plans for good and not for evil, to give you a future and a hope" (Jeremiah 29:11, TLB).

I have come to love that verse because hope makes all the difference. Learning to relinquish Larry completely to God enabled me to face another (actually the same) parenthesis and know I could get through. I had said, "Whatever, Lord," and I had meant it!

After Larry left, the Spatula ministry began to take off. I'd share on television and radio shows, or I would speak in churches and conferences and people would ask, "Well, how is your son now?" And I would have to say, "Well, he's disowned us. He's changed his name, and he says he never wants to see us again."

That wasn't real hopeful news to share, but it was true at the time. All I had to hang on to was a love for God and a love for Larry and all those parents who had suffered the loss of a child or the pain of having a child reject their values and opt for a different lifestyle that leaves God out.

Real Hope Comes Out of Hopelessness

I identify with the woman described in the following poem from Ruth Graham's book *Sitting by My Laughing Fire:*

> She waited for the call
> that never came; searched every mail
> for a letter, or a note,
> or card,
> that bore his name;
> and on her knees
> at night
> and on her feet

all day, she stormed Heaven's Gate
in his behalf;
she plead for him
in Heaven's high court.
"Be still and wait,"
the word He gave;
and so she knew
He would do in, and for,
and with him,
that which she never could. Doubts ignored,
she went about her chores
with joy; knowing, though spurned,
His word was true. The prodigal had not returned
but God was God,
and there was work to do."

For me, that describes hope. Hope is the essential ingredient to make it through life. It is the anchor of the soul. The Lord is good to those who hope in Him. If your hope is gone, it can be rekindled. You can regain hope—you can refocus your view and wait on the Lord to renew your strength.

The title of this chapter may be puzzling you. How can you feel better if you've given up hope? What it means is, once you give up hope in all your *own* efforts and quit depending on your *own* strength, that's when you can start to have REAL HOPE in what God can do!

Think of your life, with all the mistakes, sins, and woes of the past, like the tangles in a ball of yarn. It's such a mess that you could never begin to straighten it out. It is such a *comfort* to drop the tangles of life into God's hands and then LEAVE THEM THERE. If there is one message I want to share with you, it is to place your child, your spouse, your friend, whomever it might be, in God's hands and *release* the load to Him. God alone can untangle the threads of our lives. WHAT A JOY AND COMFORT IT CAN BE TO DROP ALL THE TANGLES OF LIFE INTO GOD'S HANDS AND THEN SIMPLY LEAVE THEM THERE! That's what hope is all about.

Hope Is Not Dodging Reality

Holding on to hope doesn't mean that we have our head in the clouds, pretending our troubles don't exit. Hope means we're trusting God to get us *through* the troubles; it's believing that the hard times will pass and that the hurts we're enduring will be healed. Hope is a lifeline to sanity, a beacon of faith we follow through the dark places that occur in our life.

You see, we just can't go through life pretending that griefs don't happen and acting like the hurt and pain aren't really there. Faith is knowing that troubles do exist, but it is also the trust to know that they're not going to last forever and that you will feel better.

Hope is the essential ingredient to make it through life! It is the anchor of the soul. But you say your hope is gone? Don't worry, it *can* be rekindled. The Lord is good to those who hope in Him.

You can regain hope; you can refocus your view and wait on the Lord to renew your strength. Those without Christ may see only a hopeless end, but the Christian rejoices in an *endless hope.*

How Do You Define *Hope?*

Sometimes it's hard to explain hope. Just what is hope, anyway? The cutest illustration of hope I've found is about a little boy who was standing at the foot of the escalator in a big department store, intently watching the handrail. He never took his eyes off the handrail as the escalator kept going around and around. A salesperson saw him and finally asked him if he was lost. The little fellow replied, "Nope. I'm just waiting for my chewing gum to come back."

If your face is in the dust, if you are in a wringer situation, be like the little boy waiting for his chewing gum to come back. Stand firm, be patient, and trust God. Then get busy with your life . . . there is work to do.

I like the note one mother sent me that simply said:

Dear Barb (and Gopher Bill): Like the sundial, this year I am only going to count the sunny hours! I don't know where we are—I don't need to know. It's all in His hands. How much safer could it be?

Her words remind me that nothing touches me that has not passed through the hands of my heavenly Father. NOTHING. Whatever occurs, God has sovereignly surveyed and approved. We may not know why (we may *never* know why), but we do know our pain is no accident to Him who guides our lives. He is, in no way, surprised by it all. Before it ever touches us, it passes through Him.

The Painful Art of Tunnel Walking

To come out of the darkness into the sunshine, it helps to remember you're in a tunnel, not a cave.

You will get through this if you just hang in there and keep on *walking through that tunnel.* I have a special friend named Peggy who often shares cards and thoughts with me, and one of the best she sent was this:

DARK MOMENTS ARE SHORT CORRIDORS
LEADING TO SUNLIT ROOMS!

One of the best pieces of advice on how to walk through your corridor or tunnel was written by Robert Maner, an evangelist who lives in Georgia. Several years ago in an article entitled "Tunnel Walking" in *Herald of Holiness,* he mentioned terrible tragedies that can happen to any of us—a wife learns that her husband is leaving her for another woman; the doctor gives the dreaded news that you have terminal cancer; an unmarried teen-age daughter says the shocking words, "Mom, I'm pregnant"; the state patrol calls saying your son was killed "while driving under the influence."

All these tragedies happen every day, and Christians are not exempt. When these things happen, there seems to be no light at the end of the tunnel. I know that feeling. You can hear Romans 8:28 quoted again and again, but it's still all dark— there is no light anywhere.

You can feel guilt, anger, bitterness, and depression all at once. You keep asking yourself, "Where did I fail? What did I do wrong?" As Robert Maner says, "Dreary days and nights seem to melt together in a meaningless twilight zone." He goes on to say that although you can't change what happened, there are some things that can help. You are a child of God, and that means you have certain rights, privileges, and resources. He writes:

Jesus will walk with you down your long dark tunnel. At first even His presence may seem far away. But if you look, and feel, He is there. Right by your side you can feel Him standing there. Suppose you had to walk this path alone? But you don't—He is actually there. You can talk with Him. Share your bitterness, your anger, your guilt. Tell Him how depressed you are. Tell Him how afraid of the darkness you are. Tell Him how lonely you are.

He provides courage in that dark tunnel life has forced you to walk. . . .

While you may see no light at the end of your tunnel, you never know when the tunnel will curve. And right around that curve may burst the light of a great new day. You cannot see it from where you are now, but it is there.

Then, too, every tunnel ends someplace. Otherwise it would just be a cave. And life is definitely not a cave for the Christian. Jesus verified that by His resurrection. Listen closely and you may hear His voice bidding you to quicken your pace.

I remember a time of tunnel walking years ago. The darkness was suffocating—so dense I could feel it. No light at the end of my tunnel could be seen. I prayed—or tried to—but I couldn't seem to get through the ceiling. Sleep was impossible, so I went outside and walked around in the night. When I looked up, the stars were all there. Not one was missing. I thought surely there would not be one left, but I was wrong. And the God who put them there was also right where He had always been. The next morning the sun rose just as it had always done. The birds were singing, too. Not even they failed me. The day came when the tunnel took a sudden and unexpected turn. There was light—

lots of light. There were answers to prayer, too. It didn't happen overnight, but it did happen.

Your tunnel will have light at its end, faithful Christian. Just keep walking.

The "Perfect Answers" Don't Work

One way to get through your tunnel is to remember nobody's life is perfect, even though commercials and TV shows like to claim it's possible. My friend Lynda was looking really sharp, and I told her so. She remarked that she had bought a new bra, and the name of it was "NOBODY'S PERFECT!" That reminded me of how many of us have to live in situations where nothing and nobody is perfect—not even halfway perfect at times.

It's easy to expect too much from people or from products that are advertised as "The perfect answer." I was in a car wash recently, and while I was paying my bill, I saw a counter display selling little bottles called "New Car Smell." On the label was a picture of a spanking-new car wrapped with a big bow on it, and without bothering to take a sample sniff, I just bought a bottle, figuring I could stand a new car smell in my '77 Volvo.

When I got home, I sprayed it around inside the car and almost got sick from the aroma that seemed to be a combination of old oil, tar, and bananas. If a new car ever did smell like THAT, the owner would surely think something was wrong.

I also remember some years back when stores carried unpopped popcorn that came in colors. The kernels were bright red, green, purple, and orange. I bought some, thinking that when it popped, we would have some truly colorful popcorn. We stood around and watched it popping, only to learn that it came out snow white as usual. The colors we anticipated never did show up.

Advertisements have a way of building our expectations, but we learn reality the hard way. No spray will make an old car smell new, and colored popcorn always comes out white. Yet, something inside of us keeps us willing to believe those ads. Maybe we're always hoping for that miracle, and that's why we always try something new to see if it does what some-body says it will—to see if we can find the perfect solution.

Life Can Turn Upside Down

But nothing is perfect. We have to live in a world that is not perfect with people who are full of quirks and in homes that have imperfections. I have a friend who saved and scrimped to buy some expensive wallpaper for her son's bedroom. It finally arrived after being special-ordered, and she brought it home and put it away, planning to hang it as soon as she found the time.

Her husband discovered the wallpaper and, while she was out shopping for the day, he decided to surprise her by hang-ing it himself. So he worked all day, papering the entire bed-room with the lovely new paper, which was supposed to show colorful balloons with the strings hanging down. He made only one mistake: he hung all the paper UPSIDE DOWN, and the strings were all pointing up the wall like slithering snakes instead of hanging down gracefully as intended.

When my friend returned, she was shocked, but it was all done and couldn't be changed. So she and her husband simply learned to live with the upside-down wallpaper and adjusted to seeing the strings going up. She had wanted it to be just perfect, but it had come out exactly opposite of what she had planned.

Learning to live with upside-down situations is not always easy, but it is part of life because we all face living with im-perfect situations.

We have a clock in our car that is always one hour off from October to April when the time changes. The mechanism that changes the dial is broken, and during those months I have to keep remembering that the clock in our car is one hour ahead of life. I have to keep adjusting my time and schedule accord-ing to a clock that is one hour off, and perhaps this is teaching me something. Some things in life are NEVER what they should be, and you have to adjust. Being willing to adjust to something less than perfect is a sign of acceptance.

One heartbroken parent, whose child had disappointed her terribly, finally came to terms with her trials. One of the things that helped her was this little essay:

ACCEPTANCE

Acceptance is the answer to all my problems today.

When I am disturbed, it is because I find some person, place, thing, or situation—some fact of my life—unacceptable to me, and I can find no serenity until I accept that person, place, thing, or situation as being exactly the way it is supposed to be at this moment.

Nothing, absolutely nothing, happens in God's world by mistake.

Unless I accept life completely on life's terms, I cannot be happy.

I need to concentrate not so much on what needs to be changed in the world as on what needs to be changed in me and in my attitudes.

— Source Unknown

I got a letter from a dear lady who admitted she had no offering to send for the Spatula ministry, but her love and prayers are with us. She said:

My husband has not worked in four years since his legs were both amputated from an accident. My son is in contact with us now, thanks to Spatula, and he has moved near us to help with the farming. I have recovered from my surgery for breast cancer, and thank the Lord for that. However, the eye problem I told you about has increased so much the doctors tell me that I will lose all my sight within a few months. But I am thankful my husband can read to me when I go blind, and he will interpret all the cartoons and jokes for me so we can laugh together when your newsletter comes each month. I have laughed more over your newsletter than all the smiles I could muster since these trials came to us. How I praise the Lord for Spatula and the laughter it brings to me, along with the encouragement to hang on when everything looks so black.

In her pain, facing problems that would leave many people distraught, this lady still has reason to hope!

God Uses Troubles to Sweeten Us

Life is never perfect, but Jesus is. And He takes the imperfections—the broken pieces and the messes—and turns them into hope. Remember, no matter what you're going through, it didn't come to stay; it came to pass. You may be living in a parenthesis, but whatever you're going through, it won't last forever.

Not long ago Bill and I were driving through Palm Springs, the famous desert resort community. We came upon a roadside stand, and the sign said, "DESERT SWEETENED GRAPE-FRUIT." I thought, *That's the way it is with all of us when we go through a desert experience—when we're out there in the barren and dry wastes, not seeming to receive any encouragement from anybody. That's the time God uses to sweeten us as we learn to give our problem completely to Him.*

There are several steps we all go through when we try to give a problem completely to God. You take your first step when life rises up to knock you flat—you CHURN. You feel as if your insides are full of knives, chopping you up in a grinder. There is no other way to describe the devastation you feel when you're churning inside.

Your next step is to BURN. That's right, you want to kill your child, and then you want to kill yourself. You are so full of red hot anger and the anguish of frustration that your temper is out of control. You literally feel as if you're burning inside.

In your third step, you YEARN. Oh, you want so much for things to change! You just ache inside for things to be as they were before you knew about this. You yearn for the happy past, and this stage often lasts the longest of all.

But then you take your next step, which is to LEARN. You

talk with others, maybe you find a support group, and you learn that you're in a long growth process. You become more understanding and compassionate. Spiritual values you learned in the past will suddenly become *real* to you. You will learn a great deal about unconditional love and reaching out to help others. The wonderful result is that you relieve your own pain.

And, finally, you take your last step—you TURN. You learn to turn the problem over to the Lord completely by saying, "Whatever, Lord! Whatever You bring into my life, You are big enough to get me through it." Now you can relinquish your heaviness to God, knowing that He is in control. He loves your child more than you do, and He has not rejected your child because of whatever is in his or her life. When you nail your problem to the foot of the Cross and say you have deposited that problem with the Lord and truly mean it, then you will be relieved of your crushing burden.

But now comes the really difficult part. Just because you've come through all those steps does not mean that you will not go back to churning, burning, and yearning on certain days. But each time you will stay in those stages for a shorter and shorter period. And you will be able to spend more of your days turning it all over to God. In 1 Peter 5:7 we are told to cast our cares upon Him. That means to deposit your cares, just as you deposit money in a bank, and leave them there. So many parents write or call me and ask, "How can we give our kids to God and find some relief for this devastation we feel?" I believe, from my own struggling, that the answers are in the stages of relinquishment I describe above.

CHURN awhile . . . BURN for a time . . . YEARN for as long as it takes to move on . . . LEARN as much as you can . . . and then TURN it all over to the One who cares for you. Don't fret if you think you are not progressing or even when suddenly, for no reason, you find yourself back at square one. You may find yourself churning, just as you did at the beginning. That is normal and very typical of grief. Never forget this is a grief process, and you have to work your way through the shattering of your life.

Right now you have a broken dream. It may not always be so, but for now it is, and you have to accept it. But believe me . . . healing does come. The mending process takes time, but you are making a long journey to becoming whole again, and you have *a door of hope ahead*! I love the way one woman signed an Easter card she sent me: "FROM AN EASTER PERSON LIVING IN A GOOD FRIDAY WORLD." Even in the midst of this messy old world, we can rejoice because we know our future—and our hope—is in Him!

 ## Extra Thoughts to Take Along

Only some of us learn by other people's mistakes;
the rest of us have to be the other people.

* * * *

When you're lonely,
    . . . we wish you LOVE.

When you're down,
    . . . we wish you JOY.

When you're troubled,
    . . . we wish you PEACE.

When things look empty,
    . . . we wish you HOPE.

— Source Unknown

* * * *

TRUE UNDERSTANDING

We do not understand:
Joy . . . until we face sorrow,
Faith . . . until it is tested,
Peace . . . until faced with conflict,
Trust . . . until we are betrayed,
Love . . . until it is lost,
Hope . . . until confronted with doubts.

— Source Unknown

* * * *

WHAT LIGHT?
I'M STILL LOOKING FOR THE TUNNEL!

* * * *

HOPE MAKES A DIFFERENCE

Hope looks for the good in people instead of harping on
the worst in them.
Hope opens doors where despair closes them.
Hope discovers what can be done instead of grumbling
about what cannot be done.
Hope draws its power from a deep trust in God and the
basic goodness of mankind.
Hope "lights a candle" instead of "cursing the darkness."
Hope regards problems, small or large, as opportunities.
Hope cherishes no illusions, nor does it yield to cynicism.

— Source Unknown

* * * *

Thank You, dear God
For all You have given me
For all You have taken away from me
For all You have left me.

— Source Unknown

* * * *

TAKE YOUR BROKEN DREAMS
TO JESUS!

5

One Laugh = 3 Tbsp. Oat Bran

BE GRATEFUL . . .

for husbands who attack small repair jobs around the house. They usually make them big enough to call in professionals.

for children who put away their things and clean up after themselves. They're such a joy you hate to see them go home to their own parents.

—Source Unknown

This chapter is "just for fun," but for a good reason. If I have learned anything through life's trials, it is this: *"A merry heart doeth good like a medicine"* (Proverbs 17:22, KJV).

A good cry is a wet-wash, but a hearty laugh gives you a dry cleaning. A good laugh is worth a hundred groans any time in any market. *She who laughs, lasts* because:

LAUGHTER IS THE SUN THAT DRIVES WINTER FROM THE HUMAN FACE.

If you can learn to laugh in spite of the circumstances that surround you, you will enrich others, enrich yourself and, more than that, you will LAST!

Laughing Is Like Jogging on the Inside

Doctors and physical fitness experts tell us that laughter is just plain good for your health. One expert, who travels around staging workshops on how to be fit, says healthy people laugh one hundred to four hundred times a day.

And I read about one medical doctor who calls laughter "internal jogging." He says that hearty laughter has a beneficial effect on most of your body's major systems—and it's a lot more fun than calisthenics. Laughing one hundred times a day works the heart as much as exercising for ten minutes on a rowing machine. When I speak, I invite my listeners to try "jogging on the inside"—having some good, long laughs in spite of the pain or frustrations in life.

One bumper snicker I saw became the title for this chapter: ONE LAUGH = 3 TBSP. OAT BRAN.

You undoubtedly know all about oat bran, the new "wonder food" that has proven to be effective in lowering cholesterol levels. Dr. James W. Anderson, who is Professor of Medicine at the University of Kentucky, and a specialist in diabetes, bought a hundred-pound sack of oat bran and began using it in his own diet. In just five weeks, his cholesterol level dropped 110 points, or 38 percent![1]

I'm not sure if laughter can lower cholesterol, but it's definitely healthy. And besides, laughter is a lot more appealing than eating oat bran, which I have found to be close to sawdust. Nonetheless, Bill and I have our oat bran almost daily. It helps diabetics control their blood sugar and also just plain reduces risk of heart attack.

Have you ever thought of how many days we waste if we don't learn to laugh? Someone said, "The most wasted of days is that in which one has not laughed." There are so many books out on how to love your family, how to succeed in marriage, how to get thin, how to get rich, how to cope, how to survive an earthquake, what to do when teen-agers run away from home, but nothing on how to learn to laugh. How often parents are told to "zip up your child and give the entire container to the Lord because there is no way out of this." But parents need to hear God can take them through whatever they're facing. And learning to laugh can make the journey so much more comfortable!

Try a Laugh Break—It Works!

I read one article that says the best thing to do when feeling overwhelmed is to take a "laugh break." If you're all worn out and feeling defeated, take time out to laugh. It can actually rejuvenate you.

In one psychological study, sixty people were divided into three groups and given equal puzzles to solve. All three groups failed the first set of puzzles. Then the researchers gave Groups One and Two some easier tests, like rearranging scrambled letters into words. Both groups did almost as poorly on this as they had on the first batch of really difficult puzzles.

Before taking the same scrambled letter test, however, Group Three was allowed to have a "laugh break."

They got their chuckles out of reading a group of ten cartoons to see which ones were the funniest; then they took the scrambled letter test and scored well. The point is, humor can actually alter your mood.

Humor made it easier for Group Three to get motivated. Their laugh break helped them overcome their earlier frustration and do a better job!

My Joy Box Grew into a Joy Room

The best way I've learned to laugh is to pursue joy and actually collect it. My books and newsletters often mention my Joy Room, a 60' x 10' space attached to my home which is full of things to make me and my guests smile, chuckle, and even guffaw. My Joy Room started out as a Joy Box—a shoe box covered with some brightly colored paper—in which I put things that made me laugh. When I was going through the really terrible times and doing my own share of tunnel walking, I looked for things like cards, poems, and even Scripture verses that made me smile or laugh. In a way, *The Love Line* newsletter is simply how I share all my joy with other people.

In the first years of our Spatula ministry, I'd go out to speak, and if I'd talk about watermelons, people would send me watermelon potholders with cute little sayings. If I talked about balloons, I got balloon potholders. In no time at all, my Joy Box was brim full and overflowing, and we had to do something else. So much joy was coming back to me in the mail, I told Bill we had to build a room on the side of our home, and that's just what we did. Today on every inch of the walls, we have plaques, pictures, dolls, and gimmicks—all kinds of happy stuff all over the place.

One of my favorite occupants of my Joy Room is a little lady in a basket, with a sign that says, "DON'T PICK ON ME. I'M A BASKET CASE ALREADY." People have also sent me all kinds of dolls and stuffed animals. A foot-high Bugs Bunny sits on a carrot that's at least a foot and a half long. He's very precious to me because he was made especially for me by a mother whose son died of AIDS. She came through the death of her boy beautifully, and because of what's happened in her life, she's reaching out to other mothers who are going through the same kind of pain. She attends our Spatula support group every month. She loves to talk or write to other mothers to encourage them.

I used to have a little blue sandman with cute red feet, a little package of sand in his hand and wearing a little hat to help him go to sleep. He was called Sleepy Sam, and I gave him to Al Sanders, host of the "Vox Pop" radio program, because Al told me he seems to always need a nap in the afternoons lately. Because we are the same age, I like to remind Al that you're over the hill when you spell relief N-A-P.

Another favorite in my Joy Room is a big, beautiful doll made by a Roman Catholic nun. About eight feet long, with stretched-out arms and stretched-out legs, the doll is so realistic that she fooled a United Parcel Service man who came by one day. Instead of his usual loud knock on the door, he tapped very quietly. He said, "I didn't want to wake up the lady." I used to take this doll along on speaking engagements. I'd put her in the backseat, and it often looked like somebody was riding with me. Sometimes I would jokingly tell people I kept her in the backseat so I could ride the Diamond Lane.[2]

Love Gifts Fill My Joy Room

In addition to all the handmade love gifts that decorate every inch of my Joy Room, I get a lot of poems and sayings from our SPATULA family. One I especially like is called "Home Rules." It was taken from a church bulletin and the original source is unknown to me.

If you sleep on it . . . make it up.
If you wear it . . . hang it up.
If you eat out of it . . . put it in the sink.
If you step on it . . . wipe it off.
If you open it . . . close it.
If you empty it . . . fill it up.
If it rings . . . answer it.
If it howls . . . feed it.
If it cries . . . love it.

One of the occupants of my Joy Room reminds me that sometimes you need to have tough love for your children. He's a little porcupine who actually looks more like a ground-hog, but he reminds me that when you love your kids, they may send back responses as hurtful as porcupine quills. That's what happened when Larry disowned us and changed his name, saying he never wanted to see us again. But all the time he was gone, we kept loving him unconditionally.

Parents must remember they can't change anybody. Billy Graham's wife, Ruth, says, "It's my job to love Billy and God's job to make him good." I've adapted that idea, and I say it's my job to love my kids, and it's God's job to touch their lives.

As someone said, we spend the first three years of a child's life teaching him to walk and talk and the next fif-teen teaching him to sit down and be quiet! But, ultimately, there are only two things you can do for your kids—love them and pray for them. So I keep my little porcupine in my Joy Room to remind me that, even though our kids may send back quills—that is, they may do or say things that sting and hurt—it's our job to love them with unconditional love, not "sloppy agape," but with a tough love that has some edges on it.

The Joy of a Serendipity

Sometimes I don't find joy; it finds me. It's just plain fun to go around speaking for women's groups in churches, conferences, luncheons—all kinds of places where women invite me in to share with them. Their creativity is astounding. Sometimes the room is decorated with little spatulas hanging down from the ceiling. Sometimes each table has a "Joy Box" centerpiece. After I wrote *Fresh Elastic for Stretched-Out Moms*, I'd go to luncheons that featured posters with limp rag dolls representing "stretched-out" mothers. In one case, a lady had set up a rag doll going through a real, old-fashioned washing machine wringer! I always come away from these meetings feeling I've received more than I have given.

Recently, I was speaking somewhere and was told that I would be introduced by a lady who had never introduced anyone before. This dear gal practiced and practiced and even made a little tape of her introduction, which she played for me ahead of time to make sure she had everything right. That night she came with a new hairdo and in a new dress, complete with a corsage. The big moment arrived and she got up and said, "We're so glad to have Barbara Johnson with us. She's written a book and in that book there is a chapter called . . ." Her face got white and I could tell she had forgotten her whole speech, but she continued bravely, ". . . there is a chapter called 'Stick a Geranium in Your Cranium'!"

I laughed so hard I could hardly begin my speech, but then I thought, *"How appropriate!"* She was trying to describe a chapter in *Fresh Elastic for Stretched-Out Moms* called, "Stick a Geranium in Your Hat," which talks about using laughter and humor to make it through the nights and days that seem so endless when tragedy and pain occur. I've always liked the idea of facing problems by looking for the flowers, not the weeds. That's why *Stick a Geranium in Your Hat and Be Happy* became the title of this book. Maybe it isn't always quite that simple, but finding happiness and joy has to start somewhere, and I know it starts with a positive attitude.

Look for Joy—It's Everywhere!

We can learn to look for laughter and joy in the many ordinary places where we go. When I go to our La Habra post office in the morning, the cement on the sidewalk outside is just plain blah gray. But if I go in the afternoon, when the sun hits it, the cement sparkles with a million transient diamonds! So I usually go in the afternoon, looking for the joy that can bounce off that cement right into my life, to remind me of the sparkles all around us if we are willing to look for them.

But I repeat, you have to LOOK for the joy. Look for the light of God that is hitting your life, and you will find sparkles you didn't know were there. Recently, a darling young mom who has four kids, all under six, called me and wanted me to come over and do some counseling with her. I said, "Four kids under six . . . would you like me to bring a baby-sitter or something?"

"Oh, no," she said, "I have a perfect solution. It'll be no problem at all."

I thought to myself that this would be interesting. I wondered what she was going to do to keep four kids under six occupied while we tried to have a meaningful chat.

I went over to her house, and we went out into the backyard. Then she took two handfuls of pennies and threw them into a large patch of ivy growing on the hill. Then she gave each of her four kids a plastic baggie and told them to look for pennies in the ivy.

What a terrific idea! We had an hour of no interruptions. And, for all I know, she does the penny exercise every time she needs some time to concentrate or talk with someone. Anyway, it's a wonderful idea because her kids are learning how to look for joy as they search for the pennies in the ivy.

Try Doing Something Truly Outrageous

I read somewhere that one way you can put more laughs into your life is to do something just plain outrageous. How

long has it been since you have done something really
GOOFY? Intentionally, I mean. Like jogging in triangles? Or
driving in circles in a parking lot just for fun? Or going to the
market wearing your wig inside out?

I had gone quite awhile without enjoying some goofy fun,
so Marilyn (my partner in crazy fun) and I decided to do
something about it. We knew of a pastor who had been having some tremendous family problems and who was feeling
down and depressed. He had said to me, "What I REALLY
need is a visitation from the angels!"

Well, that was all we needed. The next day Marilyn and I
went by our church, where we slipped into the baptismal room
unnoticed and "borrowed" two long, full-flowing, baptismal
robes. We drove over to our friend's home and stopped to don
the robes about a block from his house. A mailman walking by
nearly dropped his pouch when he saw two women get out of
a Volvo and toss on these white robes with heavy weights in
the bottom that sort of clinked as we walked.

When my husband, Bill, heard about our fun, he thought it was sacrilegious and unspiritual. His main concern was "Did you get the robes returned to the church?" But our pastor friend thought it was great. He got up in church and told everyone about these two women who came to give him a "visitation from the angels."

Laughing's More Fun with Someone Else
One thing about laughing: it's hard to do alone. You usually need somebody else to watch, listen to, or react to in some way. We can't do it all alone, whether it's laughing or anything else worthwhile. We need other people in our lives. We need other people to help carry the load. Sometimes I tell people to read the following story to their families so they can all laugh together. I don't know the original source, but it illustrates beautifully that you "can't do it alone." When one man was asked to fill out a group insurance form explaining the many injuries on which he was making a claim, this is what he said:

I am writing in response to your request concerning Block No. 1 on the insurance form which asked for the cause of injuries, wherein I put "Trying to do the job alone." You said you needed more information, so I trust that the following will be sufficient.

I am a bricklayer by trade, and on the day of injuries, I was working alone, laying brick around the top of a four-story building, when I realized that I had about five hundred pounds of brick left over. Rather than carry the bricks down by hand, I decided to put them in a barrel and lower them by pulley, which was fastened to the top of the building. I secured the end of the rope at ground level and went up to the top of the building and loaded the bricks into the barrel and flung the barrel out with the bricks in it. Then I went down and untied the rope, holding it securely to insure the slow descent of the barrel.

As you will note on Block No. 6 of the insurance form, I weigh 150 pounds. Due to the shock of being jerked off the ground so swiftly, I lost my presence of mind and forgot to let go of the rope. Between the second and third floors, I met the barrel coming down. This accounts for the bruises and lacerations on my upper body. Regaining my presence of mind, again I held tightly to the rope and proceeded rapidly up the side of the building, not stopping until my right hand was jammed in the pulley. This accounts for my broken thumb.

Despite the pain, I retained my presence of mind and held tightly to the rope. At approximately the same time, however, the barrel of bricks hit the ground and the bottom fell out of the barrel. Devoid of the weight of the bricks, the barrel now weighed about fifty pounds. I refer you again to Block No. 6 and my weight. As you would guess, I began a rapid descent. In the vicinity of the second floor, I met the barrel coming up. This explains the injuries to my legs and lower body. Slowed only slightly, I continued my descent, landing on the pile of bricks. Fortunately, my back was only sprained and the internal injuries were minimal. I'm sorry to report, however, that at this point I again lost my presence of mind and let go of the rope. As you can imagine, the empty barrel crashed down on me.

I trust this answers your concern. Please know that I am finished with trying to do the job alone.

Life Goes On—So, Laugh!

Robert Frost said he could sum up everything he learned about life in three words: "IT GOES ON!" I believe that's, oh, so true. The human spirit can survive pain, loss, death, taxes, and even a wild ride with a barrel of bricks and life goes on . . . and on and on. My encouraging word to all those I meet is "develop a sense of humor to carry you through these days. Without one, you are doomed to despair. With one, you can survive and actually enjoy the trip."

Years ago my Joy Box pulled me through the rough days when I had nothing else going for me. I felt all alone in that dark pit. I didn't know then that others had been through it and had *made* it. Collecting the poems, cartoons, verses, and all kinds of paraphernalia and knickknacks was a way to MAKE myself look for joyful things. It brought me from where *I was* to where *I am* now. I can look back and remember it, but I'm not there anymore. It came to pass; it didn't come to stay.

So my word to you today is: *Get yourself a Joy Box.* Just decorate a shoe box, and start today to collect things that are fun, cute, inspiring. When you start collecting joy, you'll find that it's like a magnet. At first a shoe box may be big enough, but soon you'll have to enlarge it to a basket. Then you'll need a barrel, and before you know it, you may have to add a room to your house, just the way we did, in order to have space for all that joy.

One thing I treasure in my Joy Room is a wooden plaque on the wall with the name BARBARA on it. Printed below that name is its meaning: "COMING WITH JOY." I'm so thankful to everyone who has made God's love abundant and running over (see 1 Thessalonians 3:12). So many have sent me care and love and turned my Joy Room into a haven where people can come to kick back, put it in neutral, and just learn to smile again. Some people who come to see me have not smiled or laughed for months, but sitting in the Joy Room is a form of therapy. Even the grandfather clock seems to chime its message, "I love you, friend, so very much!"

I feel I have earned the Joy Room. I've come back from the black pit—back into life again.

I was talking with a lady once and said: "I wonder if there is any place in the Bible where it says that Jesus laughed."

She said, "I don't know where it says that in the Bible, but I do know that Jesus sure fixed it so *we* could!"

And I thought, *She's so right. God fixed it by having Jesus die on the Cross and then raising Him from the dead. He fixed it so we could have laughter and joy, so we could look up and say, "Thank You, Lord, for what You've given us—salvation and eternal life."* And we can laugh—I genuinely believe we can laugh and be joyful Christians because of what He has done on Calvary for us.

Extra Thoughts to Take Along

If there was ever a man who knew sorrow, it would be Job, and yet in his story you find this promise from the Lord, if you trust in Him and put it all in His hands:

HE WILL FILL YET YOUR MOUTH WITH LAUGHTER AND YOUR LIPS WITH SHOUTS OF JOY.

—Job 8:21, NIV

* * * *

Sometimes I think
I understand everything.
Then I regain consciousness.

— Ashleigh Brilliant
Pot-Shots No. 423
© Brilliant Enterprises 1973

* * * *

DON'T TAKE LIFE SO SERIOUSLY—
YOU'LL NEVER
GET OUT OF IT ALIVE.

— Source Unknown

6

Guilt—The Gift
That Keeps on Giving

Lord,
There are countless things in my life
That are inexcusable.
There are things unaccountable
And things unexplainable.
There are things irrefutable
And things irresponsible.
But it comes to me with unutterable relief
That because of Your amazing love
Nothing in my life is unforgivable.

—"Beautiful Fact"
Ruth Harms Calkin

Whenever I talk to parents who have been shattered by the news that a daughter is pregnant out of wedlock or a son has opted for the gay lifestyle, I usually turn to two favorite tools: a bottle of "Guilt Away" and a windshield wiper. I actually have a spray bottle with "Guilt Away" on the label. This much-needed "product" was invented by two young men who were nursing hangovers while on a sailing trip.

They decided that they needed a modern way to get rid of guilt, so when they got back home they founded their own laboratory and started putting out eight-ounce bottles of rose water labeled "Guilt Away" for sale in stores across America.

With all that pain and guilt floating around out there, they

expected to sell at least a million bottles the first year, and I'm sure they reached their goal. But, unfortunately, a squirt of "Guilt Away" doesn't take care of guilt. The reason I hold up my bottle is to get people thinking about the *real* way to spray away guilt—with 1 John 1:9, which says: "If we confess our sins, he is faithful and just to forgive us our sins, and to cleanse us from all unrighteousness" (KJV).

Erma Bombeck said guilt is "the gift that keeps on giving," and that's so true. Too many of us—whether moms or kids—can relate to the thought I saw expressed on a sign not long ago:

*MY MOTHER WAS
THE TRAVEL AGENT FOR GUILT TRIPS.*[1]

That's why I also carry a windshield wiper when I speak—to use as a reminder that we have to wipe away the past. You can't beat yourself over the head for mistakes you've made (or you think you've made). Maybe you've had alcoholic parents or been a victim of incest. All kinds of things happen to us to cause pain and guilt, but we don't have to carry this "gift" around with us. We can say, "Lord, wipe that thought or memory from my mind. Help me think of things that are good, pure, and lovely [Philippians 4:8] as You renew my mind from within [Romans 12:2]."

God Had a Problem Child, Too!

Parents are always asking, "Where did I go wrong?" I tell them that God was a perfect parent, and look at the big mess He had with Adam! Who are we to think that we can be parents and not have big problems with our kids, too? While I was on a radio show, a pastor called in and told me he had a woman in his congregation whose son was a homosexual. The woman was extremely distraught, and he was wondering what he could tell her. I told him this:

> The first thing you can say to her is that she's not to blame. Help her to not play the blame game. God was a perfect parent, and look at the mess He had with Adam. So try to get her to see that her son's homosexuality is not her fault—she hasn't done *anything* to contribute to that. Removing the blame is the first thing that you can do, and then help her to reach out with unconditional love to her son.

For many years, psychologists have argued about what really shapes the personality: the genes or the environment. How a child is brought up by his or her parents is important, but recent studies show that the genes play a major role. Some experts believe good parents can have rotten kids and lousy parents can have super kids. Often, there is no clear connection between the way kids are parented and the way they turn out.

I run into many parents who are wracked with guilt, asking: "What did we do wrong?" when their kids seem to go haywire. It helps to tell them that much of the latest psychological research concludes that parents really can't take too much of the credit or the blame for the way their kids turn out.

I'm not trying to get parents completely off the hook of being responsible fathers and mothers who should do the best job they can of rearing their children. God makes it clear that we should "train up a child in the way he should go: and when he is old, he will not depart from it" (Proverbs 22:6, KJV). But what these psychiatrists are saying should bring some guilt relief to parents who feel they have failed completely. A lot of what our children grow up to be and do is *not our fault!* Our job is to love them, and then leave the final results up to God!

One of Spatula's major expenses is its telephone bill. I get and make calls all over the country to parents who need help. Countless times I get calls from mothers who have gone completely *bananas* over the action of their kids. I can relate to them with empathy because I've been there. All of us get over those panic feelings at different times, and I was pleased to get the following letter from a mother who tells so clearly how she faced her panic and guilt and moved back into reality:

> I got so weary after two years of waking up at 2:00 A.M. with pains in my stomach. I knew if I kept it up, I would be completely ruined. So, I "had it out" with God. I pointed out to Him that Carol is *His* more than she is mine, and that He loves her more than I do.
>
> I said, "God, *You* should take care of her. You know how to reach her where I cannot." At that time I laid down my burden and *left* it. I no longer have any guilt, for I know I was the best mother I knew how to be. I probably made lots of mistakes, but no one could ever say I didn't CARE. . . . This is my philosophy, and it has worked to get me through this terrible depression of knowing my daughter was a lesbian.
>
> Perhaps it will help some other mother who is where I was a year ago.

The Lady with Hamster Hair

Mothers go into all sorts of emotional responses when they have learned that their child is into sinful behavior of one kind or another. When I learned about Larry's homosexuality, I was flooded with guilt as well as physical symptoms like "an elephant on my chest," a "shag rug in my throat," and "itchy teeth." I ran onto one mother who completely lost all of her hair within a week of learning her son was gay. I met her at a meeting, and when she pulled off the little scarf she was wearing on her head, there were only some fine, downy patches of sparse hair, sort of like the hair on a hamster.

I tried to give her some help, reminding her that the way our kids turn out is really not under our control. I must admit, however, that I felt relieved when she put the scarf back on her head and covered up her unsightly scalp. I had no idea if she could ever grow her hair back, but recently I got a call and a cheery voice said, "Remember the lady you met with the hamster hair?"

Actually, I vaguely remembered the lady, but I could never forget that hamster hair. "Well," she continued, "I want you to know that my hair has grown out, full and thick, and today I got myself an Afro!" That was terrific news! Hair can grow out, stomach pains can stop, and hearts can be mended, although it is often a longer process to mend hearts than to grow a head of hair.

Part of our Spatula ministry is helping people learn to live with a heartache because changes are seldom in sight and long-term anxieties sometimes last indefinitely. That's why I always welcome testimonies from parents who have learned that they can trust God with all of life's problems and heartaches. We can all face tomorrow as long as we have complete trust in Him.

I hung up the phone after talking with my friend and thanked God that her Afro was a sign of restoration, of new growth, of something springing up where it was barren before. So take heart. You may have had panic signs of your own, but I'll bet you never had "hamster hair," did you? So there's always something to be thankful for. You could have become bald from all that trauma!

During a question and answer session at one conference, a woman asked me how she could help her husband let go of the guilt for the way their teen-age son was acting. I told her we all had to let go of guilt in our lives because none of us is perfect. None of us has been exactly the right kind of parent.

What the lady could do was try to enlarge her husband's

vision and let him know that God has forgiven him for his mistakes in not dealing with his boy properly. To help anyone who is dealing with guilt, you must encourage him or her to deposit that guilt in God's care and ask forgiveness. Point them to a verse like Psalms 32:1 (the following is from *The Living Bible):*

> What happiness for those whose
> guilt has been forgiven!
> What joys when sins are covered over!
> What relief for those
> who have confessed their sins
> and God has cleared their record.

Once a person asks forgiveness and says, "Lord, I made a mess; forgive me," then he or she can get on with life. The important thing is that you *don't have to live in all that guilt.* I think we just have to say we did the best we could with what we knew. From there on, the results are up to God. If you have a failure of the crop, that's up to God, too. And as you give it to God and learn to relinquish it to Him, then you don't have to keep whipping yourself with all the remembered sins. You can get rid of the guilt, which we all want to do.

One Mom Kept Calling—at 3:00 A.M.

It's funny how some of us hang on to our guilt. I had one mother who kept calling me at 3:00 A.M. because she just didn't know why Ted was a homosexual. She lived on the East Coast and she'd often call me at 6:00 in the morning (3:00 my time). She was always crying, saying, "Oh, I don't know why Ted is a homosexual."

I didn't know why, either, but she seemed to have to talk to someone, even though it was 3:00 in the morning on the West Coast. So I'd let her talk, and talk, and talk.

Bill said, "Why don't you tell her it's three hours difference so she won't keep calling at 3:00 in the morning?"

But she never seemed to be able to get that straight.

Finally, she made one more call at 3:00 in the morning, saying, "Oh, I'm just so happy. I found out why Ted is a homosexual. It's because he's the one of the five kids that I didn't breast-feed."

I told her that was good news, but I thought to myself, *Oh, good. Now that you've found THAT out, you can begin to work on your life and your marriage and quit calling me at 3:00 in the morning.*

This poor mother had to hang it all on SOMETHING, and as soon as she knew that was why, then she could get on with her life. She had been going on a little rat wheel, but once she could get off, she could look ahead to something else. I knew that breast-feeding or lack of it was not the right answer to Ted's homosexuality, but if she wanted to hang it on that for the moment, I'd let her. She needed something to help her stabilize and get on with her life. Then I was able to get her to see how she could put her problem in God's hands. Oh, yes, she doesn't call at 3:00 in the morning anymore.

Barney Was Our Lovable Little Imp

We never quite know how our kids will turn out. When my boys were growing up, I might have said that Barney, our youngest, would bring us the most grief. His real name is Dean, but when he was little he used to love the song "Barney Google, with the Goo-Goo-Googly Eyes," which he played continuously on our player piano. So we nicknamed him Barney, and it stuck.

I talked about Barney in *Where Does a Mother Go to Resign?*:

> . . . how I brought him home from the hospital on Christmas morning, all snug in a bright red Christmas stocking, which the hospital provided for all babies going home on Christmas;
> . . . how he and another little boy painted our neighbor's porch black when he was six;
> . . . how when he was nine he shut down the entire Market Basket supermarket when he dropped a dime in the checkout line and it rolled through a crack into the gear mechanism that shorted out the entire store!

. . . and how at age ten, while I was holding down a part-time job, he would alter the lists of chores I left for him and his brothers to do after school and sign them with my special trademark by putting on lipstick and blotting it on the notes, just as I always did. Because he laboriously typed the notes and then "signed" them with a lipstick kiss, his brothers and I never suspected until the day Larry complained that he had a list that was so long he couldn't possibly do it all. That's when I checked and learned about Barney's forgery scheme.

Fortunately, Barney was a charmer and that helped us put up with all his shenanigans. When he hit high school, I thought we might have some real problems, particularly with losing two of his brothers. He was ten when Steven died in Vietnam, and when Tim died, he was fifteen.

I think Tim's death was the hardest for him to take because he was very close to Tim. I doubt that I was much help to him at that time. I probably wasn't any help at all because I spent so much time crying at the dump, trying to work out my own grief. Frankly, I didn't really worry about him. He seemed to handle it all pretty well, and besides he had turned into a Pillsbury-all-purpose-type kid. Anything was fine. He'd eat anything. Do anything we asked—no problem—except for the traffic tickets.

Before Barney was eighteen, I had to go to court with him *twenty-two times* for traffic tickets. A few of them were for speeding, but most of them were dumb little tickets that he'd get for not having the right equipment on his dirt bike. So we kept going to court in Pomona, which meant spending most of the day there. We would go up in the morning and sit there, and sit there, have lunch, then go back and sit there some more, waiting our turn.

Finally, we would talk to a commissioner, and he would say, "Now, you're not going to do this again, are you? You have a nice mother who comes up here with you, but next time we're going to take your license or impose a fine."

Barney would flash his charming smile and say, "Yes, sir, I'll never do it again!"

Well, Barney would soon get *another* ticket, and we'd go in and see *another* commissioner. Fortunately, we never seemed to see the same man twice in a row, so Barney never did lose his license—he never even got fined. Whenever I see Barney now, I tell him he owes me a two-week vacation for all that time I spent going with him to court. He's married now, and his lovely wife, Shannon, played a big part in bringing him to a total commitment to Christ. They have two lovely daughters, Kandee and Tiffany. Their home is truly dedicated to the Lord, who has done wonderful things for them and through them.

My "No U-Turn" Caper

Recently, any guilt I felt over Barney's antics when he was younger boomeranged in my face when I made one of my daily runs down to the La Habra Post Office, which is right next to the La Habra Police Station. As I came out of the post office, I noted a big sign that said, "No U-turn," but because I was in a hurry, I just made a beautiful, sweeping U-turn to get myself back in the right direction as quickly as possible.

I hadn't gotten half a block when a police car came up behind me, siren blaring and red light flashing. A lot of high school kids were going by, and so there I sat in my car as they pointed and chanted, "YEAH! YEAH! YEAH! YEAH! YEAH!" when the police officer walked up, pulling off his gloves. I hadn't had a ticket in years, but I remembered that's just how they do it. They stand there and just pull off their gloves, one finger at a time while you sit there and perspire (gently, of course). He finally got them off and said, "Didn't you see the 'No U-Turn' sign?"

I told him of course I'd seen it, but I "didn't think they really meant it."

The officer was not impressed, so while the high school kids kept staring and snickering, he stood there writing up a ticket. All the time I just wanted to get out of there. Finally, I took the ticket, stuck it in my glove compartment, and pulled away from the curb. I got about two blocks down the street, and suddenly I heard a siren again. There in my rearview mirror was a police car with the big red light going around. I thought, *My goodness, I've only gone two blocks. What have I done now?* I pulled over again and up came the same officer, pulling off those gloves, one finger at a time. Then he asked, "Do you have the original ticket I gave you?" I reached in the glove compartment and gave him what he had given me.

"No," he said, "don't you have the original?"

"Am I supposed to get more than one?" I asked. "That's all I have—that's all you gave me."

"Well, I have to have the original," was all he would say. He looked around in the backseat of my car where I had all my SPATULA stuff and finally decided I didn't have his original. So he told me to have a nice day and let me go. I put the copy back in the glove compartment and drove off. I wasn't going to tell anybody about this ticket, especially Bill, because he doesn't ever get them, and this was the first one I'd gotten in years. I didn't know what I was going to do about the ticket. I thought I might go to AAA and they could help me somehow.

Several days went by, and I knew it was about time to think about doing something about that ticket.

Then in the mail came a letter addressed to my husband, "Mr. William H. Johnson," from the La Habra Police Department. The letter said, "Dear Mr. Johnson: You can disregard the ticket that you got for making the U-turn in La Habra because the original was lost."

When Bill saw that letter, he became practically paranoid.

"What's this? I didn't get any ticket. How come I'm getting this? MY NAME IS ON THIS!"

Bill knew he hadn't gotten a ticket. But I let him stew awhile. Why should I relieve his guilt? Then I finally told him, "It's not your ticket; it's my ticket."

All he could say was, "You deserve it; you're always doing that."

He heaped all this guilt on me, which I knew he'd do, and

that's why I didn't want to tell him at first. I got a little ruffled and said, "If we all got what we deserved, we all deserve to go to hell, but it's only by the grace of God that any of us escape."

That profound bit of theology quieted him down a little, but it didn't do a whole lot for my guilt feelings, so that week I went out and bought a big box of See's candy and took it down to the police station. I didn't want to tell them who I was, because it's like getting shot at and missed when you get a ticket and then the police lose it! But if I gave them my name, who knows? They could look it up and perhaps find my ticket. So I just laid the candy on the counter and said, "Have a happy day," and left.

When I got home, I thought I'd call Barney and tell him what happened. After twenty-two tickets of his own, he might be interested.

I got Barney on the phone and told him the whole story—about getting the ticket for the U-turn and how the letter had come saying they had lost the original so I could ignore the ticket completely.

"How could that be?" Barney wondered. "I've had twenty-two, and they didn't throw any of my tickets away."

I couldn't resist. I just had to say it: "Well, Barney, if you really LIVE right . . ."

Barney just laughed, but there's a little postscript to this story. Not long afterward, we were leaving on a trip by car and stopped by his home. We went in and tried to say some hurried good-byes to Barney, Shannon, and their little girls, but just before we left, Barney said, "Oh, you can't go yet. We want to pray for you."

So, this big, 6'2" kid of ours grabbed our hands, pulled us all into a little circle, and prayed for our safety on the trip! I am sure he and his little family have prayed for us often—probably daily—but somehow, to stand in that circle of six people and have my baby son praying for us really brought the message home to me. We had come full circle. All the years of praying for our kids . . . having them dedicated to the Lord . . . teaching, training, loving, caring . . . watching them break our hearts and then seeing their growth and how the pattern of God's weaving in their lives comes out . . . all this has paid off! As somebody said, "Kids are not a short-term loan; they are a LONG-TERM INVESTMENT!"

Barney Taught Me Something about Guilt

I used to think I'd have to be nice to Barney because he would be the one who would pick out my rest home, but now that I have diabetes and am probably not going to need one, I don't have to be so nice!

One thing Barney has taught me is that condemnation only heaps up more guilt. When Bill and I learned of Larry's homosexuality, Barney told us that he had known about it for quite some time. But being the nonjudgmental type, he had said nothing. "Live and let live" was his approach, and when I look back, I can see the wisdom in that.

But I was trapped into being a mother, a parent who was supposed to uphold her standards. I couldn't accept a homosexual son. I would rather see him dead first! I became a guilt-ridden Christian, sure that I had made some bad mistakes that caused Larry to be the way he was. And then I made an even bigger mistake by rejecting him and judging him. But when I said, "Whatever, Lord," as I drove up that viaduct to commit suicide, I not only relinquished Larry to God, I handed over all my guilt as well and knew real forgiveness for the first time in eleven months.

I relinquished it ALL to God—Larry, my own failures, and whatever the future might bring. I was able to reach out and accept God's cleansing forgiveness and stand clean before the Lord! Many parents suffer needlessly because they do not deal with their guilt and receive the freedom to live *guilt free.* I found a little poem that I display on the wall in my Joy Room:

> Dear God
> I have sinned
> Against Heaven
> And against You.
> I am no longer worthy to be called Your child.

Child, I know . . . I know . . .
But My Son
Is forever worthy
To be called Your Savior.

— "Forever Worthy"
Ruth Harms Calkin

That poem tells me that God believes I am worth loving—
so are you. We are worth loving, even with our sins, even with
that which is degrading to look at about ourselves. Even with
our faults. Even with the shameful past.

Even with our rebellion.

The Good News is that you can stop nailing yourself to a
cross because Jesus was nailed to a cross for you. If you accept
His forgiveness, you can live a guilt-free life from here on out.

Over four hundred years before Christ, a Greek poet said:
"Even God cannot change the past." In a way, he was right.
What has happened has happened, and there is no going back
and changing it. But in another way, he was, oh, so wrong.
God changed the past when He sent His Son to die on the
Cross for our sins.

That provided the only possible way your sinful past and
mine could be erased. And that's why 1 John 1:9 makes sense.
That's why you can keep coming to God, asking forgiveness.
Whenever we sin, we have an advocate with the Father—His
Son, Jesus Christ. (See 1 John 2:1.)

We Are All Treasures in His Hand

The opal is a beautiful stone, but when it lies in a jeweler's
case, it's cold and lusterless, with no life in it. But let the jeweler
pick it up in his hand and the warmth of his touch brings out the
brilliant hues and colors. Likewise, when we hold the Lord at
arm's length and refuse to let Him work in our lives, there is no
brilliance, no color, no depth to living. But when we allow the
touch of the Master's hand, His love warms us and we know we
are jewels for His kingdom. Until then we are hidden treasures.

You may have seen the picture of the little boy saying, "I

know I'm SOMEBODY . . .'cause GOD don't make no JUNK!"
That little boy has a better understanding of God's love and
forgiveness than many adult parents do. Their self-esteem has
been destroyed because of something that's gone wrong in the
family. Guilt has destroyed their self-esteem, and they feel
worthless. I know that feeling—I felt it for eleven months
without relief, and I still feel it occasionally when I momen-
tarily forget I am very special to God.

One of the most fun gifts I have ever received for my Joy
Room is a shiny red ceramic plate on which is engraved: "You
are special today!" You may have heard of these red plates.
They come from a custom among Early American families.
When someone deserves special praise or attention, that per-
son will be served dinner on the red plate.

What a great idea for giving honor to a special person
with a visible reminder of your love. But the best thing about
the red plate is that it reminds me that I am special today to
God, even if it isn't my birthday, or Mother's Day, or any
other holiday. God loves me every day, and *I am always special
to Him.*

I take no more heavy guilt trips, because Jesus has wiped
my slate clean. He cannot see my sin because it is covered by
His blood. He gave me a white robe of righteousness, which
is kept clean by a special detergent called FORGIVENESS.
Because Christ is in me, I have the hope of glory, and because
of Him I deserve this special plate *every day of my life.* Anyone
who comes to visit me and my Joy Room will see my red plate
proudly displayed for all to see. I admire it often, just to make
up for all the years when I didn't have it to remind me how
special I am to God.

How I wish I could reach out to everyone—parents as well
as their rebelling children—and give each one a shiny red
plate like I have. I want to remind you of how special you are
to me and to God—you are a very important SOMEBODY in
His sight. Life is too short to be paralyzed by guilt, so accept
His forgiveness and go forward with your life, determined to
do your best.

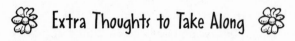

Extra Thoughts to Take Along

RELAX

If we weren't meant to keep starting over . . .
would God have granted us Monday?

* * * *

GOOD HOUSEKEEPING

Lord, it is not the dirt and clutter in plain sight that nag
   at me.
It's that hidden dirt . . . you know, behind the
refrigerator, in the closets, under the bed.
Dirt that no one sees or knows about but me.
It's the same way with my life, God.
It's those hidden sins that I can't keep up with . . . those
   petty little grievances, the grudges, the resentments,
   the unspoken harsh feelings, the superior attitudes.
Thoughts and feelings that no one else knows about but
   me . . . and You, God.
Help me, Father, to clean my heart as I would my home.
Take away all dust and cobwebs of pride, ill feelings and
   prejudice.
The dirt behind my refrigerator will never hurt anyone.
The dirt in my heart will.

—Source Unknown

* * * *

TO GET A FRESH START, DO THESE EIGHT THINGS:

1. Be born again.
2. Accept God's forgiveness.
3. Freely forgive others.
4. Learn all you can from your mistakes.
5. Turn your weakness into your strong point.
6. Accept what you cannot change, and with God's help, turn it into something beautiful.
7. Put the past behind you.
8. Get up and begin again.

—Source Unknown

* * * *

GOD'S "GUILT-AWAY" PROMISE

"Therefore, there is now no condemnation for those who are in Christ Jesus." (Romans 8:1, NIV)

1

One Day I Shall Burst
My Buds of Calm and Blossom into Hysteria

Life generally looks better in the morning.
It's just that morning takes so long to get here!

The problem with stress is that it comes at you from every direction, anytime, anywhere. I was in Texas to speak at a huge banquet, and as I started toward the podium, one lady grabbed my arm and said, "Don't step back too far because there's a hole in the carpet and you're liable to catch your heel in it."

Okay, I would be sure not to do that. I continued toward the platform when another lady, who had arranged all the flowers, whispered, "Don't push on the podium. The flowers may fall over!" That sounded a little like the guy at the book table earlier in the evening who had told me, "Don't lean too hard when you sign your books because the table collapses very easily."

By the time I got to the "danger zone" known as the podium, I was already pretty well stressed out for the evening. But just before I began to speak, I saw the maintenance man headed my way, bringing me a glass of water. *How nice!* I thought. *At last something positive.* But as he placed the glass on the podium, he delivered the *coup de grace*: "Be careful—the last speaker we had spilled her water into the microphone and almost electrocuted herself."

Somehow I continued with my talk and, fortunately, my heel never caught in the carpet, the flowers didn't fall off the podium, and I never even touched the water, so we all had a good time anyway.

When Real Stress Is a Constant Companion

Of course, THAT kind of stress is nothing to the kind I hear about in letter after letter from totally stressed-out moms and other stretched-out folks who write to me every month. They are going through *real* stress, and I always include one or two letters in *The Love Line* newsletter each month, just to let readers gauge their own progress in getting out of the pit. I empathize with these letter writers because I've been an occupant of the pit myself, and I know that it helps to read about how others are going through the same kind of emotional struggle. It all doesn't seem so unreal when you hear about someone else who has stress for a constant companion. One woman wrote to say:

> Dear Barbara and Co-Workers:
> As always, I enjoy your newsletters thoroughly—don't know how you come up with so much new material every month. I know God is with you every day, for you to keep on hanging in there with such hope and prayer for us hurting parents. It's been five years for me, and some days I think I can't live through another. I still live in constant prayer and hope for a change. I still cry at the very thought of this happening in my family, and I will never, never understand. I don't think any of my family suspects—at least they don't let on. I dream of moving far, far away where nobody but God would know.

Another mom agonized:

> These times have been horrible, and I sometimes wonder if there will ever be any relief. At the present time I am feeling numb and I cry over the dumbest things. Maybe it will not take so long, but I will keep praying. . . .

Still another letter I got simply said:

Help! Please help! My son came out of the closet and put me in it!

One mother sent a desperate plea that put me under stress:

Please send us tapes for guilt-ridden parents (us). My husband is on the verge of a nervous breakdown, and I'm a close second. Please be selective in your choice of tapes—my husband doesn't need any more condemnation nor do I right now. Although I'm more prepared than he. My son is homosexual, and we still have one daughter at home who doesn't know yet. We need help and right now. You are our only hope.

"Bad Stress" Is My Specialty

These letters come from women who are under what the medical experts would call "distress," or bad stress. There is another kind of stress, called *eustress*—the good kind of stress we all need to have just enough pressure and adrenaline flowing to help us get things done and enjoy life. But my mail bag is full of "bad stress"—the kind that can rip you apart if you let it suck you in. As one definition puts it, "stress is that confusion created when one's mind overrides the body's desire to choke the living daylights out of some jerk who desperately needs it."

I had a bad stress day myself recently when I took out a nice, new, shiny, powerful vacuum cleaner that I had just purchased. Having wielded my dependable old model for thirty years or more, I thought I knew all about vacuums and didn't bother to study the directions on operating the new one. Instead, I attached the power nozzle to the machine, already anticipating the whir of power as my new vacuum would perform for me.

Of course, I should have been suspicious when I saw a dial that indicated whether the dirt to be picked up was "FINE, MEDIUM, or COARSE." Fine dirt, I assumed, would be like silt or sand, and with my sandbox days long since faded into yesterday, I knew I could skip that setting.

But what about "medium" dirt? That might be raisins, cookie crumbles, or anything ordinary shoes might bring in. And "coarse" dirt? That could be peach pits, dirt clods, or stray Legos the grandchildren leave behind. Making a quick tour of the house, I found no collection of marbles or Tinker Toys lying loose, so I felt it was safe to set the dial on "medium dirt." Somehow I felt a little smug and proud, being able to set MY vacuum for medium dirt rather than coarse.

The indicator was set, the machine was plugged in, the bag was securely closed. I clicked the "on" button, and that began my day of disaster!

Within a few minutes, the long pedicels from a hanging plant which I had been coaxing along for several months disappeared into the machine, along with pieces of dirt clods, and green vines that had been attached. One entire side of the foliage on my plant was gone—sucked into the mouth of my hungry monster!

Before I could recover, my new extra-long telephone cord made a whirring noise as it disappeared and wrapped itself in tangles inside my voracious vacuum. I managed to disentangle the cord, but noted that chunks of the rubber covering were now missing, the holes making a regular pattern like huge teeth had clamped down on it.

And, of course, Bill should have known better than to leave his shoe in plain sight of the vacuum. In a few seconds, the tongue of the shoe was sucked up as well as the shoelace! Oh, well, I reasoned, the shoes were old and should have been discarded anyhow. But right after the shoe episode, my eyes grew wide with horror as the new Sony adapter cord for Bill's stereo headphone set wrapped itself noisily into the vacuum brushes.

So far, my plant had been eaten, the telephone cord had been mutilated, Bill's shoes were declared unfit, and now his Sony adapter was almost completely destroyed. If only we had a dog, I could blame the disappearance of the adapter cord on a teething puppy. I wondered how long it would be before he noticed his adapter cord was gone (completely eaten by the vacuum, except for the plastic head whose size alone saved it from being sucked into the nozzle as well).

Being the melancholy perfectionistic type that he is, Bill soon missed his Sony adapter cord and began checking all the electrical outlets, thinking he might have misplaced it. Finally, my conscience forced me to break my silence.

Shamefully I had to admit my POWER vacuum had sucked up his precious Sony cord and that I had immediately ordered another one (which would take several weeks to arrive).

We're ALL Like My Vacuum

I learned a lot that day. It's funny how the wording on a little plastic dial can inspire your thoughts. But we're all like vacuum cleaners, really. We all suck up a certain amount of dirt along the way. I wonder if people who absorb only "fine dirt" get special recognition? What about "medium dirt" and "coarse dirt"? Every one of us must fit into some category on that dial because it's impossible to walk through life without getting soiled. There's filth everywhere—even on TV and in gossip, idle chatter. And what about our consumer culture, which makes materialism and greed sound like the only way to live? My new vacuum cleaner prompted me to sift through my own life, looking at areas where various degrees of dirt needed cleaning out.

I discovered that part of that dirt was stress. And I realized that being too busy and rushing about doing more than God wants me to do is dirt that I shouldn't be carrying.

The day following the rampage of my vacuum monster, I heard the gardener outside using his tools to keep our grounds clear of debris. But instead of *sucking up* the dirt, he was *blowing it away. As* he moved along the walkways, his blower whisked away anything in its path, and I was reminded of a book I had just finished reading, *Blow Away the Black Clouds* by Florence Littauer. It's a terrific book on dealing with depression. And one of the things that makes it so terrific is that it DOESN'T depress you!

I thought about my power vacuum and how we can spend our lives sucking in the dirt, absorbing it, taking it up, and putting it in a neat little bag to be disposed of later. But with that method, you're always collecting more and more. The gardener had a better approach. He simply blew all the dirt away and left a clean path where he walked. All the crevices and walkways were clean, and he didn't have the added worry of what was fine, medium, or coarse, either.

Are You Absorbing Too Much Stress?

I think there is a real application here to how we live. We can absorb and soak up a lot of crud and collect a lot of misery. We can hold on to the pains that are bound to come, almost cherishing them. We also do this with depression and other crummy stuff. We can cling to this until our bag is full, and then we may dump it—usually on somebody else.

Or we have the option of blowing all that negative thinking away—the criticisms and grudges, the self-depreciation that leads to compulsive behavior designed to please others. We can ask God to remove it completely, replacing darkness with His light, sweeping us clean of unforgiveness, bitterness, greed, and social ambition. He can make a springlike freshness in our hearts if we will know and practice the presence of the Holy Spirit.

Where are you today? Are you going through life sucking up grudges and grievances that turn into pressure and stress as you remember all the wrongs done to you? Are you carrying around other bagfuls of dirt from old sin areas? We often have the mistaken idea that stress is something other people and outside forces cause in our lives. Stress can be caused by external factors, but very often *we cause our own stress.*

We can let God blow away our stress—get it out of our path, out of our lives. Then we can stand clean before Him with the assurance that He can keep us from losing our minds. Not only that, but He can help us renew our minds daily.

You Can't Control It All

Something that helped me cope with my stress instead of continuing to collect it along with a lot of other mental barnacles was realizing that *If there is no control, there is no responsibility.*

Dr. Harold Greenwald has co-authored a book called *The Happy Person.* He believes there are at least six realities in life that we can't change and we must accept. Getting older is one of them. Getting old is inevitable, but according to Dr. Greenwald, if you consider the alternative, it is a process you can learn to enjoy. (More on that in chapter 9.)

Also, there are always things in life that will not be fair. And there will be some people who won't like you no matter how kind, good-natured, and charming you might be.

You must keep in mind that life is a constant struggle. Some people think that if they can just get over the particular hump or through the particular tunnel in which they are struggling now, that everything will be smooth sailing from then on. That just won't happen. Better to see life as a series of problems that are opportunities to learn and grow, and then you won't get nearly as stressed out when the struggles come.

Above all, remember that you can't change people. That was a hard one for me because I always wanted to change Larry. But I had to let Larry do his own changing, with God as his motivator and power source. Once I stopped trying to change him, most of the stress went out of our relationship.

Use Laughter to Cope with Stress

With all its pain and problems, life is no joke, but as I explained in chapter 5, learning to laugh can help you cope. I agree completely with the professor of psychology who believes laughter is the best way to relieve stress and get yourself in a new frame of mind. In an Associated Press release (I don't know the date), Dr. Robert Leone of United States International University said, "When you're laughing your attention is focused. You can't do anything else. Everything else, whether it's depression or stress, stops."

Dr. Leone also says a good laugh can cleanse your emotional state and make you feel better about going on. He lists all kinds of ways to put a little more laughter in your life:

1. Try listening to a humorous record by one of your favorite comedians, or go see a funny movie. It's a temporary lift, but just the release of laughter will make you feel better.

2. Try expanding your activities. For example, maybe you never sing in the car because you don't want people next to you on the freeway thinking you're weird. Try it sometime, and then you can chuckle over the funny looks you get.

3. Quit making excuses for why you aren't happy. "At some point," says Dr. Leone, "you have to take responsibility for your own happiness. People . . . settle for 60 or 70 percent happiness, but they could be a lot happier."

Singing Can Work Wonders, Too

I mentioned above that singing in the car might produce some weird looks and a few laughs, but there are even better reasons to sing. I often sing as I ride my exercycle, take showers, or do housework. The experts say you can live longer with a song in your heart. In one case, doctors put twenty professional opera singers, ages twenty-eight to sixty-five, through eight minutes of rigorous breathing exercises. Every singer did it in a breeze, but a group of forty nonsingers *under forty years old* struggled to finish the test and their heart rates soared.

Psychiatrists sometimes urge their patients to sing away tension and anxiety. When you sing, you get rid of energy, and this can take your mind off your troubles, spark pleasant memories, and ease physical tension.

Try singing in the shower to get ready to face the day or singing in the car, especially when traffic is bumper to bumper. Pick songs that are inspiring and motivating. For me, hymns and gospel songs do that the best. Some of my favorites are "Amazing Grace" and "When Answers Aren't Enough, There Is Jesus."

How to Survive the Rat Race

One of the major causes for stress in daily life is PRES-
SURE. Recently I met Tim Hansel, author of a great book on
dealing with pain called *Ya Gotta Keep Dancin'*. We were both
invited to speak at the same conference, and I got a chuckle
when Tim said, "I'll bet both our schedules are somewhere to
the left of WHOOPEE!" That reminded me of one of my
favorite bumper snickers:

> *JUST WHEN YOU THOUGHT*
> *YOU WERE WINNING THE RAT RACE,*
> *ALONG COME FASTER RATS.*

We all have to run the "rat race." The trick is to try not to
drop out of the race, but to pace ourselves so we can LAST. I've
learned to be thankful for my diabetes because it has forced me
to avoid stress and eat properly. I look at it as a positive
thing—something that's good news instead of bad.

God's Advice for Defeating Depression

It's important to deal with stress because it can easily turn
into depression. In fact, I once read an article that said depression is often caused by *not learning how to deal with the stresses*
in your life. Women especially have to be on guard because
their personalities tend to make them more prone to depression than men.

From my own experience, I agree. Almost every week I talk
to depressed mothers who feel like the bull's eye on the dart-
board of life. Many of them just want to curl up and find a
hole to hide in (which is what I did the first time Larry left for
the gay life). But I urge them to try to keep busy, to keep
going. And I also tell them to be patient. It takes time to get
over depression, but it does end. It doesn't come to stay; like
much of the other pain and hassle in life, it comes to PASS.

I found a wonderful paraphrase of 1 Corinthians 13. It can
be a real help, particularly if you're feeling down and
depressed. Try reading this paraphrase aloud every morning

and evening, and the realization of God's love will start seeping into your life to blow away your black clouds:

BECAUSE GOD LOVES ME
(BASED ON 1 CORINTHIANS 13:4–8)

Because God loves me, He is slow to lose patience with me.

Because God loves me, He takes the circumstances of my life and uses them in a constructive way for my growth.

Because God loves me, He is for me. He wants to see me mature and develop in His love.

Because God loves me, He does not send down His wrath on every little mistake I make, of which there are many.

Because God loves me, He does not keep score of all my sins and then beat me over the head with them whenever He gets the chance.

Because God loves me, He is deeply grieved when I do not walk in the ways that please Him because He sees this as evidence that I don't trust Him and love Him as I should.

Because God loves me, He keeps on trusting me when at times I don't even trust myself.

Because God loves me, He never says there is no hope for me: rather, He patiently works with me, loves me, and disciplines me in such a way that it is hard for me to understand the depth of His concern for me.

Because God loves me, He never forsakes me even though many of my friends might.

Because God loves me He stands with me when I have reached the rock bottom of despair, when I see the real me and compare that with His righteousness, holiness, beauty, and love. It is at a moment like this that I can really believe that God loves me.

Yes, the greatest of all gifts is God's perfect love!

—Source Unknown

Stress Is in the Eye of the Beholder

I learned from personal experience that one person's "stress" is another person's minor irritation. I can still remember when

I was going through my black tunnel of despair and a lady called me to tell me her problem. It seemed that she had "fat pads" on her knees. My own heart was so raw and bleeding that it was all I could do to listen patiently to her complaints. But to her, the fat pads were an all-consuming problem, and she had to talk to someone about them.

Another woman wrote to me about a similar situation she experienced, saying that she had gotten so frustrated she let off a little steam, which she later regretted. She wrote:

> Once a lady in my class asked for prayer because her husband would not pick up his socks. I said (and I am ashamed of it), "Would you like to trade places with me? I have a bad heart, a retarded son, and an alcoholic husband given to sporadic violence. I have an illegitimate grandson. A man my husband fired threw a Molotov cocktail into a warehouse we had just filled with roofing materials on credit, causing the second largest fire (our city) ever had. We had no insurance. After three years of struggling to pay for the burned stock, the recession forced us into bankruptcy. And people tell me to lose weight when we are living on beans and potatoes."
>
> I was immediately ashamed because the lady had all she could handle with the sock problem, and playing "Can You Top This?" gives the Lord no glory. I have learned a lot over the years, usually too late.

How true! We do learn a lot over the years and often it seems to be too late, but it's never too late to face stress and hassles with a positive attitude. Something can always be done to straighten life out, no matter how full of twists and snares it gets.

Under Stress at a Rescue Mission

I still say the most positive thing you can do about stress is to learn to laugh. Recently, I was invited to speak at the Los Angeles Rescue Mission on Skid Row. That was stress in itself because this isn't my usual audience. Bill had come with me, and because he had a bad cold, he sat up on the platform behind me nipping at a little bottle of cough medicine. Of course, it looked as if he was nipping at something else!

As I was trying to get into my talk, I noticed one man in the front row who had his hat pulled way down around his ears. Just then, one of the mission workers came down the aisle with a long pole. It was almost twenty feet in length and had some kind of gripping device on the end. He reached the pole clear across the front row and snatched the man's hat, plucking it right off his head, then turned and walked out. The Union Rescue Mission has a strict rule—no listening to speakers with your hat on—but I guess they had no rule about throwing speakers for a loop by reaching across the row with a twenty-foot pole and plucking off hats. Nobody seemed to notice, though. Everybody just kept listening to my story, which was at a very serious point. And all the while Bill kept sitting behind me, nipping away at his cough syrup.

At a moment like that, you have to decide, "How am I going to react to this?" Well, I just answered my own question. "Hey, this is too ridiculous to cry about, so I might as well laugh." And that's just what I did. The stress drained away, and I got through the talk okay.

On the Way—Not Yet Arrived

But even with all the ways I cope with stress, there are still little incidents that remind me I haven't completely arrived. It has been several years since that night at the flagpole in Disneyland, and while I have come far, I have not yet arrived. I still struggle with shocked feelings and flashbacks that bring tears. The strangest things can trigger me. For example, once I was in a local travel bureau looking at vacation folders. Suddenly my eye caught the following words on the front of a cruise ship folder: IS CRUISING REALLY FOR ME?

Before I knew anything about homosexuality, those words would have been no threat, but now that I had been "educated" in gay jargon, I knew that "cruising" doesn't always mean enjoying oneself on a luxury liner. Suddenly, all the old feelings of shock rushed back. My chest began to feel heavy, my throat got dry, my stomach felt like peach pits were churning around scraping the inside raw. Suddenly, I was back in the turmoil of that first day when I learned about Larry's homosexuality. Insane as it might sound, once again everyone looked gay to me.

I share this incident to help you understand that you will have yo-yo experiences. You may think you are making progress and then WHAM! You see one folder in a travel bureau (or something else), and you are right back to square one! The simplest things can trigger those feelings all over again. You feel you are getting some control over the crying and the outbursts, and then for the slightest reason you come unglued, and you feel as if the bottom has dropped out.

But when stress like this hits, remember you're in a long, tough process. We all take a couple of steps forward and then take a step back once in a while. But there is healing and there are *gains*. This, too, will pass, but oh, so slowly!

The setting of one of my favorite cartoons is also a travel bureau. A lady is standing at a counter, talking to her travel agent who obviously has just asked, "Where would you like to go?" Her answer: "Some place where troubles melt like lemon drops away above the chimney tops."

I love that. That's just where you and I would like to go, too, but unfortunately, we have to cope with life as it is. I am with all of you out there who are still fractured. I understand the yo-yo syndrome and what stress can do to keep you on it. Through years of struggle, my mind has learned a lot, but emotionally I am still fragile and need God's glue to keep my mind centered on Him.

When stress closes in, your best move is to turn to the Lord. "Take a new grip with your tired hands, stand firm on your shaky legs" (Hebrews 12:12, TLB). And laugh as much as possible. It will keep stress under control, and it also accelerates the healing of your fractured mind!

Extra Thoughts to Take Along

*OF ALL THE THINGS I'VE LOST,
IT'S MY MIND I MISS THE MOST!*

* * * *

If only I could get that wonderful feeling of accomplishment without having to accomplish anything.

> — Ashleigh Brilliant
> *Pot-Shots No. 431*
> © Brilliant Enterprises 1973

* * * *

*TODAY IS THE TOMORROW
YOU WORRIED ABOUT YESTERDAY,
AND ALL IS WELL.*

* * * *

THE TIME IS NOW

Lord, I see with startling clarity
That life is never long enough
To put You off
Until tomorrow.
The things that are before

Are all too soon behind.
I can never pick up
The years I've put down.
If I intend
To walk with You tomorrow
I must start today.

—Ruth Harms Calkin

* * * *

I DON'T KNOW THE ANSWERS,
BUT I KNOW SOMEONE WHO DOES.

* * * *

NEW BEGINNING

O God,
What shall I do?
I am at the total end
Of myself.

Wonderful, dear child!
Now start your new beginning
With Me.

—Ruth Harms Calkin

8

I Married Mr. Wumphee

*Never criticize your spouse's faults; if it weren't
for them, your mate might have found someone
better than you.*

—Jay Trachman

My husband and I are very different people, a fact you have
no doubt already observed. They say opposites attract, and in
our case it seemed to happen on our first date. We started the
evening with different partners (I had set him up with a girl-
friend), and by the time we came home, Bill was with me and
my friend was with the guy I had started out with.

When Bill and I got married, I didn't know anything about
temperaments. I didn't realize that being talkative, emotional,
demonstrative, enthusiastic, cheerful, and bubbling over with
a good sense of humor meant that I was basically Sanguine.
And I'm sure that Bill, who is deep and thoughtful, analytical,
serious, sensitive to others, and conscientious, had no idea
that he was pure Melancholy.[1]

All I knew was that Bill seemed steady, calm, faithful, and
devoted. Something in me responded to that. Intuitively, I
knew I needed someone like Bill to balance my own tendency
to be too excited, all helter-skelter, and disorganized. And I
think Bill sensed he needed me to offset his tendency to take
life too seriously. So we got married and learned that, while
opposites attract, they also must *adjust* to each other. The only
real point of this chapter (except to tell you some funny stories
about Bill) is this: *You have to learn to accept people as they are
(especially husbands).*

115

I'll never expect Bill to be as happy and bubbling with enthusiasm over things as I am, and he has finally decided I'll never be as orderly, methodical, and organized as he is.

So we have spent several decades adjusting to each other and building a strong marriage based on acceptance. Bill is really a great guy; he's just terrific, but I've had to learn that with his melancholy temperament he's what I call a "sinker"—not a "stinker" but a *SINKER*. Let me give you an example.

Recently we had a beautiful smog-free day, which is getting pretty rare in Southern California. The sky was azure blue, and the clouds were fleecy white. I looked up and said, "Wow, it looks as if God vacuumed the sky."

Bill looked up and said, "Yeah, but He'll probably dump the vacuum bag tomorrow."

Bill doesn't see a glass just half empty; he sees all the smudges and water spots, too. Order and precision are all-important to him. He wants the checkbook to balance, and he likes his sandwiches made so that the bumps on the bread fit together perfectly. Sometimes I like to tease him by trimming off the edges of the bread so he never knows if the bumps matched or not. These things are important to him.

The other day he got a new key ring and spent almost an hour putting all the keys on the ring so they would all face the "right" way. He says he can't use my key ring because I have the keys jumbled every which way.

Stapled Socks Are Safe Socks

Bill's idea of real fun is stapling his socks together when he puts them in the wash so they won't get separated. He started doing this when our boys were growing up, so his socks wouldn't get mixed up with any of theirs. Being the type who would never staple anything together, I tried to rationalize it by remembering that Bill had been in the navy; and besides, he's an only child, and they're all a little strange anyhow.

I mentioned Bill's stapled socks at a conference somewhere, and, afterward, one gal came up and told me her husband not only stapled his socks, but he marked them "1" and "2" so that he didn't get his big toe in the wrong sock!

I Laughed 'Til I Dried

One thing I must be constantly aware of is that what is funny to me is often not funny to Bill. Awhile back I was in Atlanta to do some speaking, and afterward I hurried to the airport to catch my plane for home. I had already checked my luggage and was sitting in the waiting area expecting to board in a few minutes when the loudspeaker said, "All DC-10 flights have been shut down for at least three days." I went up to the counter and was told that my flight was a DC-10; therefore, I wasn't going anywhere for a while.

I called Bill and told him I wasn't coming home, that they were going to put us all up in a hotel, and we'd be there for two or three days. Bill suggested that I just relax and enjoy the chance to rest, but I reminded him that it would be hard to relax without any luggage.

They shuttled us over to a hotel near the airport, and I checked into my room. Because I was going to be there two or three days, I did what any sensible woman would do—I washed my pantyhose, washed my slip, washed my face, and got ready to go to bed. I had *nothing* with me. My luggage had already gone to California (I hoped), and that was it.

Just as I finished washing my pantyhose and slip and they were drip-drying in the bathroom, I got a phone call. It was the airline saying, "If you can be here in twenty minutes, there is a flight leaving. But if you don't get that flight, there is nothing out of here for three days. It will be the only flight going out of here to California."

"Hold that plane!" I shrieked. "I'll *be* there to make the flight!" Then I saw my dripping-wet pantyhose and slip. I quickly rolled them in a towel and tried to get as much water out as I could, but it really didn't do much good. If you've ever tried to get wet pantyhose on a dry fat body, believe me, it's not easy!

And then there was my slip. That didn't go on very well,

either. Somehow I managed to wiggle into the pantyhose and slip, but that meant that my feet were soaking wet and I had to try to get them into my black suede heels. I dashed downstairs, dripping puddles everywhere, and grabbed a taxi. He got me to the airport in record time, and then I ran down the long concourse to the plane, dripping all the way. I made it to the gate just as they were closing up and getting ready to pull away. And, of course, when I sat in my seat, I left another big wet mark because I was still soaking wet.

When I got home, I told Bill the story, and he just cringed. He was humiliated to think that I might have left a wet spot on the plane seat. I told him, "The seat wasn't much of a problem; you should have seen all the water I dripped down the concourse to the gate!"

I had chuckled all the way home on that flight. I thought the whole thing was really funny, but Bill just found it embarrassing.

His and Hers Peanut Butter Jars

One thing that drives Bill crazy is a "messy" peanut butter jar. He doesn't like me to plunge into the peanut butter with my knife and make a big mess. He thinks peanut butter should be smooth, and when he gets to the bottom of the jar, he likes to scrape every bit of peanut butter up until the jar is so clean, it looks as if it's been scrubbed. THAT makes him really happy.

Sometimes he'll go out to the kitchen to make a sandwich and bellow, "Who has been in the peanut butter?"

Since there's nobody living there but the two of us, he knows the answer. Who else would be in the peanut butter but me? Then he makes me feel so guilty because I plunged into the peanut butter jar too deep and messed things up.

I finally solved all this by buying a big jar of peanut butter for him and a big jar for me. Now I just plunge in any old way I want to!

I have lots of women come up to me after I speak and say, "I think my husband must be your husband's brother, or at least a distant cousin. He's just like that." Maybe your husband is, too. You see roses; he sees thorns. You see God vacuuming the sky; he sees God dumping the vacuum bag. You're planning the next party, and he's worrying about all the trash the party will make; in fact, he worries about all the trash in the whole world, plus the shortage of water, the national debt, and any number of other serious matters. And the bottom line is, he *likes* to worry about all that stuff!

How Bill Became "Mr. Wumphee"

Somehow our marriage has always worked because I simply tell myself, *That's the way Bill is, and that's what he's going to be.* And I'm sure he says the same about me.

Years ago he started calling me "Cumphee." I decided to come up with a nickname for him and finally settled on "Wumphee." People sometimes ask me what Wumphee means, and I say I'm not sure. Do pet names for your husband really have to MEAN anything? All I can say is, "He's just a Wumphee—and I like to have him around!"

A couple of years ago, I got my personalized S-P-A-T-U-L-A license plate, which caused any number of comments. Once I parked in an improper place (probably while hurrying into the La Habra post office) and someone called out: "Mrs. SPA-TOOLA! You can't park there!"

I was having so much fun with my S-P-A-T-U-L-A license plate, I decided that Bill needed his own personal plate, too. And I had the perfect name for that plate: W-U-M-P-H-E-E. Back then we both drove Oldsmobiles. Mine was a late model, and Bill's was a 1974 Delta 88, which he picked up when an elderly man in our mobile home park died and his widow didn't need the car anymore. It was in immaculate shape and took regular gas, which appealed to Bill no end because he wouldn't have to fool around with smog certification.

Whenever you want to order a personalized plate, you have to check to be sure someone else doesn't have that name already. So I went down to the Department of Motor Vehicles and got out their giant book, which lists all the personalized plates in California. As I sat there in the DMV office, lifting the heavy plasticized pages, which couldn't be ripped or torn and which were permanently marked, I came across names like S-T-R-E-I-S-A-N-D, S-I-N-A-T-R-A, and S-E-L-L-E-C-K. And then I saw the name S-P-A-T-U-L-A (my car). And then it hit me. Just as S-P-A-T-U-L-A is in the giant permanent DMV book, my name, Barbara Johnson, is in the Lamb's Book of Life and can't *ever* be erased!

It was like God wrapped me in His warm comfort blanket to assure me that I was His child . . . that my name was *forever* in His Book. It cannot be torn out . . . it cannot be defaced. Once you are born into God's family, you are permanently His. There are no abortions in God's kingdom. When you are born into His river of life, you may get off into some eddy or into a little tide pool. But you are still in the river, and God always considers you His own property.

If you've ever been to the DMV, you know that it's a place without many sparkles, but that day God brought me a special sparkle, and I was so excited at the prospect of my name in His eternal Book that I nearly went up to glory right then and there!

As you may have guessed, nobody else had a WUMPHEE for his personalized plate, so I ordered it. Then I dashed home and excitedly told Bill the whole story. I shared how blessed I was when I saw SPATULA in the DMV book and realized that my name—and his—are written in the Lamb's Book of Life. But Bill just gave me a blank look and didn't get excited at all.

When the plates arrived, Bill did put them on his Delta 88, but without much comment. I thought my present was a bust, but then one day, not long after, he called me and said, "I'll be late getting home because I'm going to get Wumphee some new shoes."

"What do you mean?" I wanted to know. "You don't need a new pair of shoes."

"No—I mean the car—I'm going to get new tires for my car. Wumphee needs new shoes!"

Now, for Bill, this was pretty lively as far as putting humor into the conversation. Of course, I laughed and told him how funny that was. It seems that after getting the new plates for his car, Bill had pulled into this certain station where he buys all his gas, tires, and other things for the car. When the attendants spotted his license plate, they started calling Bill "Mr. Wumphee." From then on it was natural to start calling his car "Wumphee" and to talk about buying it things like shoes.

He also covers Wumphee up from time to time with a car cover, and when he does, he talks about "putting Wumphee's coat on," just as you would for a person.

It's Hard for Men to Cope with Feelings

During those eleven months when I was counting roses on my bedroom wallpaper, weeping continually, and feeling so little self-esteem I started thinking about suicide, I became a burden that Bill didn't quite know how to handle. Frankly, he was not a lot of help to me, and of course, I was of no help to him. For a long time after we discovered that Larry was a homosexual, Bill kept saying, "It's a phase—just a phase." Further down the line, he realized it was more than just a phase, and then he said, "The pendulum will swing." I wasn't sure what that meant, but now that our estrangement is over and we have a good relationship with Larry, he says, "The pendulum has swung." And that was about the extent of Bill's insight.

As I travel around the country speaking, I talk to many gals who ask me how Bill helped me during my times of depression. I have to tell them that, in my experience, men are not a lot of help because they don't have the emotional makeup to experience the depth of emotional pain women do. A man will hurt, but often he has no way of expressing this or letting it out. Most men don't seem to have the ability to empathize with the kind of problems their wives go through. They love their wives, and they want to help, but they just don't seem to know how to say the right things. While I was doing my tunnel walking, Bill didn't know what to say, so he did the next best thing: he took care of a lot of little chores that I detest and dislike.

For example, he kept my car clean and filled with gas all the time. He organized my kitchen cupboards and lined all the kitchen drawers with heavy vinyl linoleum. He organized my audiotapes for me so that I could find them quickly, and he built special shelves in my office to organize other materials. He helped me in so many small ways, not with *words*, but with *action*—anything to help me feel my life was in order while my mind was in turmoil over homosexuals, especially during those first months.

Of all the calls I get on the telephone, I'd say 99 percent are from Christian mothers who have problems. They want to talk to anybody who can help them. In many cases, their husbands are engineers or some other kind of cognitive, unemotional type. Engineers handle numbers and mechanical things very well because all that fits together very neatly. But when they have a kid who doesn't fit into their puzzle, they don't know what to do. They just can't handle it. So men tend to go off and do their own thing. They lose themselves in their job because they just don't know how to communicate with their wives at the emotional level.

I'm not saying that men can't communicate at all. It's possible that some husbands can give a wife spiritual help and even a certain amount of "good, practical advice," but there is an emotional level that few men can understand when it comes to a woman's feelings. God just didn't make them that way. And a wife only frustrates herself when she tries to get her husband to feel what she wants him to feel emotionally when he just isn't on that wavelength.

What almost always happens is that the woman feels isolated

and alone. She and her husband have this "problem child," but she gave birth to the situation—the problem came out of her body. And, believe me, it is a problem to understand how homosexuality fits into a Christian family.

Usually when the husband feels guilty, he blames someone else. In the case of a homosexual child, that someone else is almost always the wife. His wife feels guilty, too, but she usually blames herself, and they're both caught in the "blame game."

As a rule, men cannot face the emotional failure of having produced the problem. They generally refuse to even talk about it. What happens then is that the husband is usually able to move on and do his thing, but the woman is stuck in her awful hole of depression. And because she can't open up and talk, it all remains a secret and tends to make her all the more ill. I often say, "Openness is to wholeness as secrets are to sickness."

In our case, Bill just didn't feel the guilt that I felt, or at least he wasn't admitting it. And he didn't seem to have the same desire to get Larry back and work everything out. He didn't have any of those feelings, and that's why he was able to say it was all "just a phase" and be able to live with that.

It's no wonder that a lot of women I know feel as if they live in a vacuum. They are home alone all day in their "empty nest." The kids are gone, and their husbands are out working, playing pool, or maybe just stapling their socks in the next room. This kind of woman has no one to talk to. No wonder she watches soap operas and talk shows. She's starving for any kind of emotional input because she's not getting any from her husband.

Often, this kind of syndrome causes big trouble in the marriage. The wife wants to talk about why she has all these feelings, and the husband doesn't want to hear why she has all these problems. He'd rather go work with his computer or change the oil in the car. I believe that's why experiencing tragedies, such as having a child die or having a child disappear into the gay lifestyle, often wrecks a marriage and causes it to wind up on the rocks of the divorce court.

So what can a woman do when she faces this kind of horrible black pit—a tunnel with no light anywhere? My counsel to women in this predicament is to FACE FACTS. Your husband is not going to change and become different. He is set in a kind of cement—a hardening of the attitudes, so to speak. First, you have to decide you will quit trying to change him. *Accept him* for what he is, and quit blaming him for not being able to give you the emotional help you need.

Second, you need to *find alternative ways* to get that emotional help. Develop three or four avenues through which you can get your emotional needs satisfied. For example, try tape cassettes or good books—they can really be good friends. Best of all, however, are women friends—someone you can talk to. My best advice is to locate a sister or friend going through the same pain and just talk it out—*drain the pain together.*

Not until I had my "whatever, Lord" breakthrough about Larry was I able to fully understand that there are areas where Bill just won't change. No matter how emotional or distraught I get, his melancholy characteristics will always be there. So that's why I say a wife must learn to adapt. Sometimes it's a simple solution, like buying another peanut butter jar. But no matter what you do, a sense of humor is vital. Keeping a sense of humor will save many sinking marriages.

The Case of the Lost Motel

Once you learn to adapt, you can appreciate your husband's good qualities. I certainly appreciate Bill's. Maybe I really know what "Wumphee" means after all. Maybe it's my way of saying that Bill is kind and caring and dependable. He often travels with me, which helps no end to keep me from getting lost because I'm not the greatest when it comes to directions. But as long as Bill's around, I never worry; he just gets me there.

On one recent speaking trip, we drove up to Felton, California, a little town near the Mount Herman Conference Center, which is about fifty miles south of San Francisco near the Pacific Coast. One of Felton's major features is a big intersection with one road going to San Jose, one to San Francisco, and another to Stockton. There's also a river and some train tracks.

Bill had just had his wisdom teeth pulled and was under strict orders from the doctor to keep ice packs on his mouth to prevent any possible hemorrhaging. That meant we couldn't stay up at a speaker's cabin on the conference grounds because there wasn't any easy access to a steady supply of ice.

So, instead, we checked into a little motel near the river where he could get crushed ice and maybe some popsicles to help keep his sore gums cold. We got a room with a little refrigerator and got Bill all settled in with plenty of ice, but we never did find any popsicles.

It was late afternoon by then, and Bill decided to take me up the road to the Mount Herman Conference grounds where I was to speak that evening—a "dry run," as he called it. We made that run twice, and I felt pretty confident that I could drive the five miles to the conference grounds alone that evening.

When I left around 7:00 P.M., it was still light, and as I drove to the conference grounds, I thought, *This is no problem at all.* I had a great time talking to over three hundred women that evening. By the time I left to go back to the motel, it was just after 9:00; the sun had gone down, and suddenly the road was dark and not at all as familiar as it had been when I had driven up.

When I got down the hill to Felton, I came to the big intersection and didn't know which road to take. I saw one sign that said "Stockton," but that didn't look right. Then I looked the other way and there was "San Jose." No, that wasn't it, either. Finally, I had to try something, so I turned and started down a road that I hoped was right. After a few miles I came to a sign that said, "Scotts Valley." I thought, *We never came through here. This isn't the right road, either! What was the name of that motel, anyway?* I had forgotten; in fact, I wasn't sure I had actually ever seen a name on the place—it was sort of old and run-down.

So I fumbled in my purse for the motel key and frantically inspected it, only to see, "P. O. Box 6, Felton, CA." By now I was getting pretty desperate. What was the name of that motel? I just didn't know!

As I came back into beautiful downtown Felton, it was getting close to eleven o'clock, and the sidewalks had definitely rolled up. Up ahead there was a bar with its neon sign blinking brightly on the otherwise dark street. I was so desperate I went in and blurted out: "I left my husband in a motel, and now I can't find it."

"What's the name of it?" the bartender grunted, looking at me a little strangely.

"Well, I don't know. All my key says is P. O. Box 6."

"Where are you from, lady?" was his next question.

By now I was almost choking and was sure that the man thought I was a little crazy. I managed to sputter, "I'm not from around here; I'm from Southern California. And I left him there because he just had his wisdom teeth out, and he needed to be near some ice. Now I can't find where I left him. But I do know there was a river and some railroad tracks and a health food store across the street because we went over there to see if we could find him some ice."

"You might try Highway 9," the bartender said, and he pointed me in that direction. When I got back to my car, I was glad the bartender hadn't come outside to give me directions. There on the front seat was LONG LENA—my big stretched-out doll. If the bartender had seen LENA, he would have known for sure I had escaped from a local "home for the bewildered."

I drove out Highway 9, or whatever it was, with huge redwood trees looming on both sides of the road, my headlights piercing through the pitch-black darkness. As I came around a curve, I saw someone standing in the road, waving his hands. At first I couldn't make him out, and I thought I had better zoom on by because what kind of guy tries to wave down women in cars at eleven o'clock at night on dark roads? But then I saw it was Bill! He was just standing there, matter-of-factly, waiting for me! As I pulled up and rolled down the window, he said, "I just *knew* you'd have trouble."

Relieved to hear his voice, I asked, "How long have you been standing out here?"

"Well, quite awhile. You were supposed to be through speaking at 9:00, and now it's *only* 11:30!"

I looked over and there was the motel—but no sign on it anywhere. It wasn't my fault! How was I supposed to know the name of the motel when it was nowhere to be seen?

Bill wasn't upset, just relieved that I had finally gotten back. Since that little episode, he bought me a gadget that is a combination compass and directional finder so I can better tell if I'm going north or south, or left or right. How thankful I am that I have someone in my life who cares that much for me—to stand out on a dark road for over two hours waiting to flag me down because he "just knew" I'd have trouble finding my way back.

But that's Bill; he enjoys taking care of me and watching out for me. Sometimes when I go out speaking and he's not with me, I come home with my trunk full of stuff I've tossed in every old way. He gets a lot of pleasure out of saying, "Oh, what a mess you have," and then he organizes all the books, facing them the right way, and gets everything in exact order and categorical—that's important, to have it in categories. He enjoys grumbling about it at first and muttering things about how I throw stuff all in a heap. Then, when it is all organized, he'll say, "Now your trunk is ready to go on the next trip."

I Don't Dare Leave Home without Him

When I have to fly out of town alone to speak, Bill usually takes me out to the airport to be sure I get my luggage checked correctly and get on the right flight. He also has to check the Joy Box items I take along, as well as my boxes of books. Bill usually does all that, and he's very good at it. But on a trip recently, I didn't have my melancholy husband with me; I had Lynda, who is every bit as Sanguine as I am.

So there we were at the Ontario, California, airport just talking away, having fun. The plane was supposed to leave at

12:50, but we were there early and had *plenty* of time. All of a sudden we looked up, and it seemed as if there was nobody left in the airport. I said, "Lynda, where has everybody gone?" It was 12:55! We had been sitting there laughing and talking and hadn't heard anyone announce the plane or anything. We ran down the ramp and there was the plane, almost ready to pull out. They had already made the last call. So we frantically dashed for the door and just made it, lugging all our carry-on stuff and wondering where all that time had gone.

Later, I called Bill and admitted, "I sure missed you today. I nearly didn't make the plane."

He chuckled and started chiding me, "Well, if you would pay attention to what you're doing, you'd be okay. If I could have been there, that wouldn't have happened."

So I told him that that just made me appreciate him all the more, and I'd never try to catch another plane without him. "When you're along," I said gratefully, "I can just sit and relax, and you'll get me on the right plane on time."

Why We Make a Great Team

A couple years ago when Bill retired, he became the official "gopher" for Spatula. Even though he's a competent mechanical engineer, Bill loves doing the menial, mundane tasks. It's important that things be done right. Together we make a great team, and we even sign *The Love Line* newsletter together—"Barb and Gopher Bill."

I once got a letter from a darling Spatulander who was eighty-two years old:

Dear Barbara and Gopher Bill:

As I write your names, I'm thinking I wouldn't let Bill call himself "Gopher!" So, I stopped to look in the dictionary and found it is a sort of ground squirrel—ugh. The next thing I learned is that Minnesota is named the Gopher State. Now *that is* coming up a little. Then as I read on, I found a gopher is a zealously eager person—an errand boy, assistant, or the like! The humorous spelling for this is "gofer." And lo and behold, the name fits him to a "T." Now it makes sense. He is a *Gentleman* Gopher and a *Glorified* Gopher. He is also a *Generous* Gopher because he went overboard on the matter of accessories for your stationary bike—a helmet even! I'm so glad you are "saddled" with such a nice Guy!

So am I! We *are* different people, but that's what makes us tick. I create and initiate and flutter around, while Bill follows through, organizes, and keeps me pointed in the right direction. We each have our own gifts, and because we accept those gifts, they work together to help and encourage a whole lot of other people. I can't say it better than Bill did recently when I invited him (as Mr. Wumphee) to the platform to share as I was closing my talk to a large group of women in Arizona. Here's what he said:

> It always amazes me to see what the Lord has done in our ministry together . . . how He's put the two of us together and has come out with what we have. But the thing I've learned more than anything else is that the Lord has given each of us certain spiritual gifts, and it always surprises me to see the things my wife has in the way of gifts—being able to communicate and counsel and talk and write. I appreciate being able to come along with her. The Lord has been able to put the two of us together so that we complement each other and don't subtract from each other.

And that just about says it all. I married a Wumphee; he married a Cumphee, and we wouldn't trade for anyone else!

🌸 Extra Thoughts to Take Along 🌸

When a man has children, the first thing he has to learn is that he is not the boss of the house. I am certainly not the boss of *my* house. However, I have seen the boss's job, and I don't want it.

— Bill Cosby

* * * *

What's so remarkable about love at first sight? It's when people have been looking at each other for years that it becomes remarkable!

— Source Unknown

* * * *

A perfect wife is one who doesn't expect a perfect husband.

— Source Unknown

* * * *

The ages of woman:
   In her infancy she needs love and care.
   In her childhood she wants fun.
   In her twenties she wants romance.
   In her thirties she wants admiration.
   In her forties she wants sympathy.
   In her fifties she wants cash.

— Source Unknown

* * * *

There are no perfect marriages for the simple reason there are no perfect people, and no one person can satisfy *all of* one's needs.

— Cecil Osborne
The Art of Understanding
Your Mate

9

Wrinkles Are God's Little Way of Saying ... "I'm Stepping on Your Face"

You really know you're getting old when
you bend over to tie your shoes, and you wonder
what else you can do while you're down there.

For two hours I had been doing the talk show, and I had told my radio host and all the people who had called in just about everything I knew. We were almost out of time when the host turned to me and said, "Barbara, we have just two minutes left. If you could say one thing to encourage all the people who are listening, what would you say?"

I felt a twinge of panic. I wasn't sure I could even think of my name, and I had already said everything I knew—I couldn't even think of a Scripture verse. I glanced into the little Joy Box I take with me when I'm interviewed to see if there was anything left among my props that might give our radio audience some encouragement. Then I gleefully found a bumper snicker I hadn't used, and I said, "Well, there is one thing I would like to tell everyone, and it's this: 'LIFE IS HARD, AND THEN YOU DIE.'"

The shocked host of the show looked at me as if I had lost every marble I had.

"Well ... uh ... Barbara ... maybe you could tell us in a few seconds why you think that's encouraging," he stammered.

I could tell my host was thinking, *What is she going to do NOW? I* wasn't sure either, but I plunged in.

"What I mean is, our *exit* from this life is our *grandest entrance* up there. This life isn't it! There is pain and suffering . . . but those who want to name it and claim it are looking in the wrong place because there is nothing here to name and claim! *This isn't it!*

"This life is hard. There are all kinds of pain, all kinds of problems—AIDS, divorce, crime, disease . . . sin. Life is hard, and some of the people listening know how hard it can be. But I like what my little granddaughter told me: 'Grandma, you shouldn't say life is hard and then you die; you should say life is hard and then you *get to die.'*

"I really believe that's good news for Christians. We have an ENDLESS HOPE, not a HOPELESS END, and while life is hard, someday we will die, which isn't really bad—it simply means we'll leave this life and go to be with our Lord and Savior, and what could be better than that?

"That's why I believe in rapture practice . . . I go out in the backyard and jump up and down, practicing for the rapture, because one day we'll soon be *out* of here. I love that song, 'I'll Fly Away,' because I know my future is so secure with Him. This life holds no charm for me . . . my deposits are in heaven, just waiting for me to come! What a day it will be when we cast our crowns at His feet. This life is just a veil of tears, but earth has no sorrow that heaven cannot heal. Life is hard and tough, but it is only temporary . . . this life is only a vapor, but eternity is FOREVER!"

When we finished the interview, the lights were flashing on the call-in board. It seems that dozens of people wanted to talk to the lady who thought it was so glorious to die!

Billy's Book Was Encouraging, Not Depressing

From time to time I meet people who think it's depressing to hear that "Life is hard and then you die." But I don't think so. We're all getting older, and we're all going to die, unless the Lord comes first. Why not face it positively, instead of avoiding it and looking on it as the ultimate evil?

I was on a plane the other day reading Billy Graham's book *Facing Death and the Life Hereafter* (Word, 1987). The person in the seat next to me said, "Oh, what an awful book you're reading—how depressing."

I just laughed and said, "It's not depressing, it's exciting. It's a wonderful book."

"Do you have cancer or something?" my seatmate wanted to know.

I explained that we all have a life-threatening disease. We're all going to die because we're on our way out of here and it's a one-way trip. For a Christian, it's a pilgrimage, and I believe Billy Graham's book on death is one of the most encouraging I've ever read. He tells why Christians can face death with joy, not gloom. We're all going down the road very fast. You don't have to look very far in the obituaries to see that people are going every day. And if they are without the Lord, they have nothing. But with the Lord, they have eternity, eons and eons, to be with Him.

Facing death is really the ultimate triumph for a Christian. Perhaps you have a disease, and you don't recover. If God doesn't heal you physically, He heals you spiritually, and you spend eternity with Him.

As far as I'm concerned, whatever problems we're going through, we can think of them as temporary. As I said earlier, our troubles didn't come to stay; they are going to pass. And that helps you cope, whether it's cancer or problems in your marriage or problems with your children. Whatever it is, it's all temporary. And what's up ahead is going to be glorious because of the hope we have as Christians.

That's why I laugh at getting older and overweight. You can try to fight it off—and I try along with the rest of you, but the bottom line is, it won't matter. As the bumper snicker says:

EAT RIGHT, STAY FIT,
DIE ANYWAY.

I often hear that old cliché, "Women don't get older—they get better!" The question I always ask is, "BETTER THAN WHAT?"

Recently I was in a big department store looking for a night cream, and the salesclerk (she looked about fourteen to me) showed me something new called "MILLENNIUM." That sounded sort of spiritual, so I asked her what it meant. She said it had a special ingredient that made OLD skin become YOUNG!

And I thought to myself that it probably takes one thousand years to do it! The companies keep coming out with products that claim magical powers. My friend, Joyce, sent away for some marvelous stuff advertised on TV called "DREAM AWAY." You were to take these pills at night, dream away your fat, and wake up slim in the morning! The advertisement was enticing, but the product was a total failure—as you might guess.

We can hope for a miracle, but there is no simple, quick way to be young, thin, and lovely. As the years zoom by, you begin to think you're in a war to keep your mind together, your body functioning, your teeth in, your hair on, and your weight off. It can really be a chore. It's a lot like trying to hold a beachball under water . . . sooner or later something pops up or out! My favorite excuse is, "I used to be Snow White . . . but I drifted!"

I Don't Belong with "Old" People!

They say that inside every old person is a younger person wondering what happened, and that's exactly how I feel much of the time. Bill and I live in a mobile home park and many of our neighbors are retired folks. That means a lot of the people are elderly, and I often think, I *don't belong here . . . there are OLD people living here.*

Not long ago Bill and I came across the following item on a child's view of retirement (original source unknown). It seems that following Christmas break, the teacher asked her young pupils how they spent their holidays. One small boy replied as follows:

We always spent Christmas with Grandpa and Grandma. They used to live here in a big brick house, but Grandpa got retarded and they moved to Florida. They live in a place with a lot of retarded people. They live in tin huts. They ride big three-wheel tricycles. They go to a big building they call a wrecked hall. But if it was wrecked it is fixed now. They play games there and do exercises, but they don't do them very well. There is a swimming pool, and they go to it and just stand there in the water with their hats on. I guess they don't know how to swim. My Grandma used to bake cookies and stuff, but I guess she forgot how. Nobody cooks there, they all go to fast food restaurants. As you come into the park there is a doll house with a man sitting in it. He watches all day, so they can't get out without him seeing them. They wear badges with their names on them. I guess they don't know who they are. My Grandma said Grandpa worked hard all his life and earned his retardment. I wish they would move back home, but I guess the man in the doll house won't let them out.

The other day I spoke at a retirement home for women, where most of the audience used walkers and wore hearing aids. Some even slept through my presentation! I shared with them and included a little humor like: "Wrinkles are God's little way of saying, 'I'm stepping on your face,'" and another one I really like:

> GOD MADE WRINKLES TO SHOW
> WHERE SMILES HAVE BEEN.

When I finished, a lovely little old lady came up to the front and said, "Mrs. Johnson, I loved your talk about wrinkles, and I want to give you something for your Joy Box." And then she handed me a little, blue aerosol can that said, "WRINKLE FREE—Spray Your Wrinkles Away."

I went along with her just for fun and told her that I couldn't wait to get home to try it. But, of course, when I read the rest of the label, I found it was for cotton, linen, and silk—not skin.

There is not a whole lot you can do about wrinkles, although women, especially, keep trying with face-lifts, skin peels, night creams, and all the rest of it. I have a friend who's fifty years old, but she tells people she's sixty because she really looks *great* for sixty, but *awful* for fifty!

If You Don't Mind, Age Doesn't Matter

They say age is just a matter of mind; if you don't mind, it doesn't matter. Trouble is, a lot of people *do* mind. They are comforted by articles with headlines like: "LIFE GETS BETTER WHEN WOMEN HIT MIDDLE AGE." According to a study by one specialist, middle-aged women have become more confident, independent, and organized—better able to cope with life. This researcher said, "Although we didn't find that life begins at forty for women, we did find that as they get nearer to middle age, they are more complete human beings."

I suppose there's some truth to the man's findings. What a lot of us would like to tell him, however, is that life begins at forty, all right . . . it begins to deteriorate!

Women are under incredible pressure to stay looking young and beautiful. Sad to say, they learn that youth is that brief time between buying training bras and wearing surgical stockings. I often say that I'm living somewhere between estrogen and death, but somebody corrected me once and told me to say I'm living somewhere between the *Blue Lagoon* and *Golden Pond.*

There are all kinds of ways to tell you're getting older. For example:

- Everything hurts, and what doesn't hurt, doesn't work.
- Your back goes out more often than you do.
- Dialing long distance tires you out.

And, do you know why women over fifty years old don't have babies? Because they'd put them down and forget where they left them!

The Power of Making Memories

Some of our best days have been spent with our children, and I'm sure you can say the same thing. I believe a true serendipity of getting older is looking back to the times when our kids gave us so much fun—and maybe a few fits along the way.

Once when speaking to a group, I included a section in my talk about "building laughter in your walls" by making a special effort to have memorable good times with your family. A young woman came up afterward and said: "I read your book about today's experiences being tomorrow's memories. When I finished it, I told the kids, 'We're going to make some memories!' I took all kinds of pictures of my kids and put them in scrapbooks, and we even made some videos."

After describing how she made many wonderful memories, she told me about an incident with her son: "My son, Jimmy, is seven, and one day he came home from school and said, 'Oh, I don't have any homework to do. I'm going skateboarding, then I'm going to watch TV, and I'm just going to have fun because tonight I don't have any homework.'"

This mom told me she was happy for her son and let him go skateboarding. After dinner he watched all the TV he wanted, and about 9:00 he went up to bed. She and her husband watched TV until around 11:00 and were just getting ready to turn it off and go to bed themselves. She was congratulating herself on having everything ready for the next day, but as she looked up the stairs, there was little Jimmy, a forlorn figure in his jammies. Jimmy said pleadingly, "I just remembered. I have to have a salt map of Venezuela for tomorrow."

Now, almost all parents know "salt maps" are what teachers like to assign their pupils so they can drive mothers crazy. After all, it's mom who usually winds up helping the kid get his salt map together. So there they were, at eleven o'clock at night. Little Jimmy had spent the evening skateboarding, watching TV, and having a great time and NOW it was salt-map time. Mom said, "Get the salt, get the flour. Now, where's Venezuela?" And so they tore around getting all the stuff together. "Where's the blue paint? Where's the green paint?"

Her husband, of course, had gone up to bed. It was not *his* problem. He was sound asleep, dreaming of Bermuda, not Venezuela.

Little Jimmy manfully tried to help. He sat there, struggling to stay awake as he drew his version of Venezuela, while Mom scurried around the kitchen, making exasperated sounds. Finally he looked up and tearfully said, "Mom, are we making a memory now?"

As exasperated as that mom was that night, she'll never forget the salt map of Venezuela and those precious words by her little guy. And it will be a priceless memory, one that she wouldn't trade for anything. As you get older, memories are like gold. They become more valuable than a lot of antiques and other "things" that you collect. I love the following insight on memories. Somebody sent it to me from a church bulletin. I think it makes a memorable point:

> As we go through life, each of us is taking a notebook of memories, whether we put our notes on paper, or only on the pages of the mind. As we write, it is important that we note down some little things each day for that time when those notes may be our highest joy. So note the day the lilacs bloomed, the day your little son picked a dandelion for you, the day the bluebirds found the house you made for them. In this age of bigness, the big things will crush us if we forget the words of One who said to consider the lilies of the field, and be not anxious.

I'm Awfully Well, for the Shape I'm In

Of course, we do everything we can to fight off old age, but it's a losing battle. Nonetheless, we like to think we can still handle it, that we're in pretty good shape, considering. As one poet put it:

I'M FINE

There is nothing whatever the matter with me,
I'm just as healthy as can be.
I have arthritis in both my knees

And when I talk I talk with a wheeze.
My pulse is weak, and my blood is thin,
But I'm awfully well for the shape I'm in.
My teeth eventually have to come out,
And my diet—I hate to think about!
I am overweight and I can't get thin,
But I'm awfully well for the shape I'm in.
I think my liver is out of whack,
And a terrible pain is in my back.
My hearing is poor, my sight is dim.
Most everything seems to be out of trim,
But I'm awfully well for the shape I'm in.
I have arch supports for both my feet,
Or I wouldn't be able to go on the street.
Sleeplessness I have, night after night,
And in the morning I'm just a sight.
My memory's failing, my head's in a spin.
I'm practically living on aspirin,
But I'm awfully well for the shape I'm in.
The moral is, as the tale we unfold—
That for you and me who are growing old,
It's better to say "I'm fine" with a grin,
Than to let them know the shape we're in.

—Pearl Waddell

I wasn't always into exercise. I used to agree with the bumper snicker that says:

EVERY TIME I THINK ABOUT EXERCISE,
I LIE DOWN 'TIL THE THOUGHT GOES AWAY.

That's not true anymore. A few years ago, Bill bought me a marvelous indoor exercise bike and installed it in my Joy Room next to my television set and near my Kermit the Frog telephone. He even found me an old helmet out in the garage and suggested I wear it while riding my bike!

So I donned the helmet and pedaled happily away, but

eventually it got pretty boring, just pedaling and going nowhere and seeing no one. So I figured out a way that would bring me closer to everyone in my Spatula family, and I could do it all from my own bike in my Joy Room. I decided I would bicycle across the United States and never leave home while doing it. Some people would think it was crazy, but it was just plain fun for me.

First, I got a big colored map of the United States and hung it up right in front of my bike, where I could see it as I rode. Then I got some push pins and every time I covered twenty-five miles on the bike, I'd move the pin accordingly. At the rate of ten to sometimes fifteen miles a day, it took me four months to get from L.A. to Denver.

I keep my zip-coded list of friends near the bike, and when I get to a particular city, I look to see who lives there. And then I pray for those people and their particular problems and ask God to be especially close to them that day—to wrap them in His comfort blanket of love and let them feel His presence all day long.

I actually covered every state in the Union that way, even Alaska! When I knew I was in a state where the weather is cold, I'd put on ear muffs and a scarf, just to keep in the spirit of the whole thing. And if I was down in Florida, or maybe in Hawaii, I'd sip some iced tea as I pedaled along.

Some people listen to tapes as they ride, others watch TV, and some even try to read. Those schemes are all fine, but I think I've hit on the best idea of all—something that has put zing into my prayer life. As I "rode across the country," I prayed specifically for everyone in my Spatula family, and that way I strengthened my own spiritual life as I strengthened my heart and lungs.

Did I slim down any? Not much (I'm really a perfect 10, you know; I just keep it covered with fat so it won't get scratched), but my love for all those I'm trying to help grew stronger as I pedaled across the miles. Currently, I'm on my second tour of the U.S., just coming into Kankakee, Illinois. To spur me on, I keep a bumper snicker on the wall that reminds me:

BRAIN CELLS COME AND BRAIN CELLS GO, BUT FAT CELLS LIVE FOREVER!

The Moment of Driver's License Truth

Not long ago, I had to renew my driver's license, and when the new one came, I was pleasantly surprised. Compared to my picture on the one of four years ago, I had IMPROVED! The explanation wasn't difficult. Four years before I was so tight in the wringer and so far off in zombieland and what one of my friends calls "the twilight zone," any picture of me had to reflect the shock I was in from coping with my family's problems.

Perhaps you've known the embarrassment of pulling out your driver's license for identification and watching the person stare at the picture and then at you. That person is wondering, *Is this really you?* Of course, you stumble around explaining why your driver's license picture failed to show all your "true beauty." That's the typical experience, but in my case I had looked so bad on the prior license that the new one was actually flattering. That was a day that made my heart smile indeed!

Applying for that new driver's license did remind me, however, of the changes the years can bring. The typical driver's license application has spaces where you fill in your eye color, hair color, weight, etc. Isn't it strange that women leave their weight the same as it was when they originally got their driver's license at the age of sixteen? And why is it that some men have a license they got years ago that says, "Hair: Brown," when their hair has long since disappeared and they're totally bald?

Tell me, have you ever seen a driver's license that had accurate information? What about people who have one brown eye and one blue one? There is no space for that on the driver's license. Or how about women who have "convertible tops"; that is, they change the color of their hair so often, only their hairdresser knows for sure, and some weeks *she's* wondering.

Yes, the years can bring many changes, and it is often said

that, as we grow older, we develop something called "hardening of the attitudes." There is no space on a driver's license for filling in the condition of one's attitudes. But all you have to do is get out on the freeways, and you'll quickly learn that a lot of people have become hardened, and then some!

I don't want that said of me. In fact, the following words by an unknown writer are my daily prayer.

ON GETTING OLDER

Lord, Thou knowest me better than I know myself,
    that I am growing older and will someday be old.
Keep me from getting talkative, and particularly
    from the fatal habit of thinking I must say something
    on every subject and on every occasion.
Release me from craving to try to straighten out
    everybody's affairs.

Keep my mind free from the recital of endless details,
    and give me wings to get to the point.
I ask for grace enough to listen to the tales of others;
    help me to endure them with patience, but seal my lips
    on my own aches and pains. They are increasing and
    my love of rehearsing them is increasing as the years go by.
Teach me the glorious lesson that occasionally it is
    possible that I may be mistaken.

Keep me reasonably sweet; I do not want to be a saint—
    some of them are so hard to live with—but a sour old
    woman or man is one of the crowning works of the devil.

Make me thoughtful, but not moody; helpful, but not
    bossy. With my vast store of wisdom, it seems a pity
    not to use it all; but Thou knowest, Lord, that I want
    a few friends at the end. Amen.

A "few friends at the end" is all you can really hope for. Obviously, your best friend should be the Lord, but you do want some others, too. In recent years, a lot of books have been written about friendship—how to find friends, how to be a friend, and while I haven't written any books on friendship myself, I do think I know the secret. You'll find out what it is in the next chapter.

 ### Extra Thoughts to Take Along

AGE IS NOT IMPORTANT—
UNLESS YOU'RE A CHEESE.

* * * *

I think the life cycle is all backwards. You should die first, get it out of the way, then live twenty years in an old age home. You get kicked out when you're too young, you get a gold watch, you go to work. You work forty years until you're young enough to enjoy your retirement.

You go to college . . . until you're ready for high school. You go to grade school, you become a little kid, you play, you have no responsibilities, you become a little baby, you go back into the womb, you spend your last nine months floating, and you finish off as a gleam in somebody's eye.

— Bob Benson

* * * *

Life is uncertain;
eat dessert first.

* * * *

REFLECTIONS ON AGING

Remember, old folks are worth a fortune, with silver in their hair, gold in their teeth, stones in their kidneys, lead in their feet, and gas in their stomachs.

I have become a little older now and a few changes have come into my life. Frankly, I have become quite a frivolous old gal. I am seeing five gentlemen every day. As soon as I wake up, WILL POWER helps me get out of bed. Then I go down the hall and see JOHN.

Next, CHARLIE HORSE comes along and takes a lot of my time and attention. When he leaves, ARTHUR RITIS shows up and stays the rest of the day. He doesn't like to stay in one place very long, so he takes me from joint to joint.

After such a busy day, I'm really tired and glad to relax with BEN GAY.

What a life! The preacher came to visit me the other day. He said, at my age, I should be thinking about "the hereafter."

I told him, "Oh, I do, all the time. No matter where I am—in the parlor, upstairs, in the kitchen or down in the basement—I ask myself, 'NOW, WHAT AM I HERE AFTER?'

— Source Unknown

* * * *

YOU DON'T STOP LAUGHING BECAUSE YOU GROW OLD;
YOU GROW OLD BECAUSE YOU STOP LAUGHING.

* * * *

Some people, no matter how old they get,
never lose their beauty. They merely
move it from their faces into their hearts.

— Source Unknown

* * * *

WORK FOR THE LORD. THE PAY ISN'T MUCH, BUT HIS RETIREMENT PLAN IS OUT OF THIS WORLD.

* * * *

For I am convinced that nothing can ever separate us from his love. Death can't, and life can't. The angels won't, and all the powers of hell itself cannot keep God's love away. Our fears for today, our worries about tomorrow, or where we are—high above the sky, or in the deepest ocean—nothing will ever be able to separate us from the love of God demonstrated by our Lord Jesus Christ when he died for us.

— Romans 8:38–39, TLB

10

I Don't Recall Asking for Any of This

Encouraging thought for the week:
Eat a live toad the first thing in the morning, and nothing worse can happen to you the rest of the day!

I often get "encouraging thoughts" from my good friend Mary Lou, and one of her timeliest contributions came on a day when trying to help so many people who are down in the pit almost had me down there, too. I opened the envelope and here was a cartoon of a bewildered-looking woman tied hand and foot, lying on the railroad tracks. The caption said, "I don't recall asking for any of this!" As I chuckled, I thought, *That's right! I didn't ASK for any of this, but it's what I've GOT, so I'll just take my own advice and stick a geranium in my hat and be happy!*

That little envelope from Mary Lou didn't contain anything expensive, profound, or "deep," but nonetheless, it picked me up and refreshed me for the rest of the day. I think that's the secret to being a real friend—to always be looking for ways to encourage and refresh others. Proverbs 11:25 has so much wisdom. Here's how it reads in the New International Version:

> HE WHO REFRESHES OTHERS
> WILL HIMSELF BE REFRESHED.

As you refresh others, you relieve your own pain. You may be going through a painful time right now or trying to get over a tremendous loss. If so, try refreshing another person's life, and as you encourage that person, you will find that your own pain is lessened.

As I said in the first chapter of this book, pain is inevitable. The trick is to find ways to not let it turn into misery. So when someone sends a note, a card, or a clipping, or gives me a call that boosts my spirits, it prompts me to think of ways that I can refresh and encourage others in return. My question is always, "How can I help you flatten out the pain in your life? How can I help you be encouraged?" We can't remove each other's pain, but we can dilute it. That's what I believe our SPATULA ministry is all about—helping people live with the pain that is inevitable, bringing them some encouragement, joy, and even a few smiles to wash that pain away.

My Favorite Bible Character

Al Sanders, the host of "Vox Pop" radio, asked me a most thought-provoking question: "As you look over God's Word, the Bible, who would you like to be like?"

My answer was that I wanted to be like Onesiphorus, the man of whom Paul said, "May the Lord show mercy to the household of Onesiphorus, because he often refreshed me and was not ashamed of my chains" (2 Timothy 1:16, NIV). I have to admit that Onesiphorus is a somewhat obscure character. He's only mentioned once in the entire Bible, and his name sounds like a disease, to boot! But when I get to heaven, I'm going to look him up and tell him I've spent a great part of my life trying to be like him.

The Living Bible paraphrase of 2 Timothy 1:16 says Onesiphorus' visits revived Paul "like a breath of fresh air." There Paul was, awaiting execution. Everyone but Luke had deserted him. Then Onesiphorus, his old friend from Ephesus, searched everywhere for him and finally found him in chains and brought him refreshment.

Refresh literally means "to brace up, to revive by fresh air, to cool again." The Bible doesn't say what Onesiphorus did to refresh Paul, but just the fact that he took the time to find Paul was refreshing in itself. And Onesiphorus wasn't ashamed of Paul's chains. He encouraged Paul when he was weary and lonely by letting him know there was still someone who cared.

A Refreshing Note

I listen regularly to two radio programs—"Focus on the Family" by Dr. James Dobson and "Insight for Living" by Chuck Swindoll. And I have gotten so much refreshment and encouragement from their excellent insights.

Awhile back, Chuck Swindoll did an entire radio message on a man called Epaphroditus, and as I listened to his tape, he kept saying that Epaphroditus was the man who came to "refresh" Paul in prison. Now, Chuck Swindoll is one of the most knowledgeable students of the Bible anywhere, but I realized he had Epaphroditus mixed up with Onesiphorus! I had just done a little study of obscure Bible characters, and Onesiphorus was one of the men I studied. Epaphroditus did come to see Paul in prison and brought him a gift from the Philippian church (see Philippians 2:25–30). But 2 Timothy 1:16 clearly says that Onesiphorus was the man who found and *refreshed him* with his visits.

So I just couldn't resist writing Chuck a note saying, "I heard your whole message on Epaphroditus, and he wasn't the man who came to refresh Paul. That was Onesiphorus." I sent off the note with feelings of trepidation—after all who was I to question Chuck Swindoll on something from Scripture?

Shortly thereafter, I got a letter from Chuck saying:

Dear Barbara:
    Thanks for getting in touch.
    You are right—it WAS Onesiphorus, not Epaphroditus. Easy to get those guys mixed up. Just goes to show us how obscure they really were. . . .

                              Warmly and gratefully,
                              Chuck Swindoll

One of America's greatest Bible teachers was honest enough to admit he had goofed, and he *thanked* me for my correction! Now, *that* was really refreshing! "A generous man will prosper; he who refreshes others will himself be refreshed" (Proverbs 11:25, NIV). Chuck's gracious response not only refreshed me, but it inspired me to try even harder to walk in Onesiphorus's footsteps—to be a refreshing person, investing my life in others, knowing that as we refresh others, we ourselves are refreshed.

Caring or Clacking Christians?

I heard Chuck Swindoll share another refreshing thought on one of his broadcasts. He said that Christians can be like a sack of marbles—unfeeling, unloving, just *clacking* against each other as they go through life. Or, they can be *caring* people—like a sack of grapes pressing together to provide a soft, loving place to cushion and comfort each other from the hard crushes of life. There is no question what Onesiphorus was. The next time you talk to someone who's hurting and needing some comfort, decide who you'd rather be: a soft, comfortable grape, part of God's refreshing vineyard, or a hard, clacking marble, oblivious to those who are being crushed right before your eyes.

Shannon, my "daughter-in-love," heard me talk about caring and clacking Christians at a meeting and went home and drew the little cartoon strip on this page. It originally appeared in *The Love Line* newsletter, and I believe it illustrates the point better than any words ever could.

The clacking-versus-caring illustration reminds me of something Louis Paul Lehman once wrote in the Calvary Church bulletin in Grand Rapids, Michigan, where he was pastor for many years:

> Touch someone with a warm word. Warm someone with a genuine smile. Comfort another as you've been comforted (2 Corinthians 1:4). Stand by one who is standing alone. The "sympathizing tear" and the echoing laughter can each warm a cold day. Warmth, as a song, is of such character that you cannot give it without enjoying it yourself.

The body of Christ is intended to warm those who are cold. As James said, we just can't tell people, "Go, I wish you well; keep warm and well fed" (James 2:16, NIV). We need to do something about their needs, whether they're physical or emotional.

What a Week It Had Been!

Have you ever had a year, a week, or a day when you just couldn't take one more small, insignificant irritation? I had one of those days recently when I was trying to get ready to go speak at a retreat in the mountains. The water softener was out of salt, so no suds in my bath. I got a run in the last pair of stockings in the drawer, and the phone was ringing with calls from hurting people who took longer than usual to counsel. And then there were a lot of requests in the daily mail that had to be taken care of before I could leave town.

I know there are lots of bigger problems in the world, but mine had piled up and had started to get me down. All that morning I kept looking for just a little encouragement, some small *lift* to make the day less hectic. I even made a tour of my Joy Room and tried to remember previous joys, but that day it seemed as if finding joy was not going to be easy to do.

I hurried down to the supermarket to stock up on a few things I would need for the trip. Naturally, I got a *dumb* basket with the wheels that go in different directions. As I made my way to the checkout counter, I felt forsaken once again because the space for customers with under ten items was closed. I would have easily qualified for the fast checkout line, but now I had to pick from two other checkout lines loaded with women who looked as if they were shopping for the U.S. Army.

"Please, Lord!" I prayed, "I need just a LITTLE encouragement today. Can't something happen to let me know You care about all the heaviness that has settled upon me?"

Just then, a young man stepped into an empty checkout stand next to the one where I was in line and said, *"Young lady, I'll be glad to check you out over here!"*

I looked around and suddenly realized he was talking to me. Maybe it was the *young lady* part that lifted my spirits. But mostly I think it was knowing I wasn't forsaken. I believe he opened that line *just for me*, so I could whisk past all those other women with full baskets. What a simple way to be reminded of God's continual care. Joy may not always be easy to find. Sometimes diamonds are hidden in places where we can't always see their sparkle, but we have to keep on looking for them just the same.

That day at the supermarket, I was dejected and depressed and frustrated because it looked as if I would have to wait forever to get checked out of the store with just a few items, and I just didn't have time to wait that long. But the next moment I was happy, delighted, and encouraged because I was *first* in line. Not much else seemed to go right for me that entire week, but on that day at the supermarket, a little sparkle of God's care wrapped me in His love.

And a few days later, as I leafed through a magazine, a little cartoon with the words "Color me happy when I'm the first one in line" jumped out at me! It was a picture of a woman pushing a shopping cart. God was reminding me of the joy I had experienced a few days before. And I felt His comfort blanket around me all over again! I truly believe God cares for us in even the *smallest* ways so that we may have JOY abundantly!

People are hurting in so many ways, and there seems to be so many *joyless* people. Even those of us who have the deep,

abiding joy that only the Lord can give sometimes sag under
the weight of all of life's garbage. So whenever you see a grocery cart, let it remind you that, even in small ways, God can
reveal His care to you. Then you, too, can be as ecstatic as I
was when you realize there'll be those times when you are the
FIRST (and only) one in line!

Ever Feel Like Don Quixote?

Remember Don Quixote, the positive thinker who spent
much of his life jousting with windmills? Maybe you know
what it's like to feel that you are completely absorbed in fight-
ing windmills every day of your life, sort of like chipping
away at a concrete wall with a straw. I had a day like that
recently, but, when the mail arrived, there was a tape from a
pastor in Ohio whom I didn't even know. I put it in the
recorder and listened to his message, which was on "hanging
in there" and pressing on. He talked about a lot of things, and
then asked some tough questions:

Why should we keep trying . . . why should we stand up
against the stream of life? Why should we work to love the
unlovely? Why should we never give up, even when we fail?

Why should we keep on hanging in there when no one seems to appreciate our effort, and so few seem to even *know* the sacrifices our work causes us? Why should we encourage the downtrodden, those persons who have been defeated again and again . . . why should we never give up on a wayward child? Why should we keep on hanging on? WHY? WHY?

And I was wondering what he would say. Yes, *why?* It would be much easier to just give it all up and sit and rest awhile. Then came his answer, victory ringing in his voice. And what he said made my heart leap with rejoicing:

Because, someday "the Lord himself will come down from heaven, with a loud command, with the voice of the archangel and with the trumpet call of God, and the dead in Christ will rise first. After that, we who are still alive and are left will be caught up together with them in the clouds to meet the Lord in the air. And so we will be with the Lord forever. Therefore encourage each other with these words." (1Thessalonians 4:16–18, NIV)

What a hope! What a victory! What faith for living! What a way to dispel the doubts and heaviness in life! What a motivation to excel in all we do and to keep on hanging on! And what a reason to keep on loving and encouraging others. Someone sent me this in a note, and I just love it:

Love is the one treasure that multiplies by division. It is the one gift that grows bigger the more you take from it. It is the one business in which it pays to be an absolute spendthrift. You can give it away, throw it away, empty your pockets, shake the basket, turn the glass upside down, and tomorrow you will have more than ever.

I heard of the owner of a small, crossroads store who was appointed the local postmaster. But six months after his appointment, not one piece of mail had left the village. When concerned postal officials from Washington investigated, the local postmaster explained, "Well, it's simple; the bag ain't full yet."

Sometimes we Christians are like that. We think our bag has to be full before we can share love and encouragement with others. Your bag doesn't have to be full to share your blessing with others. You don't have to be wealthy to give a portion of your time, your talent, or your resources to help someone less fortunate. If your bag isn't full, it doesn't matter. Use what you have to enrich the lives of others, and you will soon find your own cup running over with joy.

There have been so many "daughters of encouragement" in my life who have brought in meals, typed endless papers, made phone calls, or just said to me, "Come to our place and just relax and be refreshed." I am everlastingly grateful for the many loyal friends who have been an encouragement to me in the SPATULA ministry, which is extremely demanding both physically and emotionally.

The Prisoners Blew Me Kisses!

I had a truly precious day a few months ago when I was invited to speak at Sybil Brand—a large prison for women in the Los Angeles area. When I was a kid, I often went with my dad when he preached in the local jails, and I would sing for the inmates. But that was years ago, and my first reaction to the Sybil Brand chaplain's invitation was, "I don't want to go speak at a prison. How can I relate to those women? I don't know anybody in prison . . . I've never been in prison . . . I don't want to go."

But Chaplain Lelia Mrotzek persisted and kept saying, "Your message will be useful."

Finally, I decided God was trying to tell me something, so I agreed to go. But when we arrived at the place, my negative feelings all came back. In a maximum security prison, they check *everything* . . . you can't take anything with you, just yourself. I brought along my helpful friend, Lynda, to give me support and encouragement, and after I heard the instructions from the chaplain just before going up front to speak, I knew

I needed all the encouragement I could get! Chaplain Mrotzek said: "When you're on the platform speaking, pretend there is an invisible wall between you and the inmates. You can't motion to the women, wave, touch them, or do anything to evoke a response."

Then she continued, "The first ten rows of women are dressed in light blue—they're not dangerous. The next ten to fifteen rows are medium blue, and they are in here for more serious crimes. The last twenty rows are in dark blue. They're the lifers and longtime inmates with big problems. But don't worry; there are guards with guns on each end of the rows so nobody can get up on the platform and bother you."

It was so comforting to hear that there were guards with guns to control all these inmates, especially the ones who "weren't very dangerous." But I went ahead with my talk and told my whole story—about Bill and Steven and Tim and Larry. As I came to the end, there were tears in the eyes of many of the women, and it looked as if I'd get through the whole thing without breaking any of the chaplain's rules. But somehow I forgot where I was and used one of my favorite comments on motherhood: "Being a mother is like getting a life sentence in prison with no hope of parole!"

I practically stopped in mid-sentence, realizing that I had probably said the wrong thing! But the gals just hooted and howled, and their response spurred me on to make another boo-boo.

I asked the women, "How many of you like to watch soap operas?" They all shot their hands up, and I heard cries of, "Yes! I do!" I could see the guards starting to shuffle nervously and rest their hands on their gun handles, but I plunged on anyway:

"It's wonderful for you to own up to it. When I speak in churches and ask Christian women if they watch soap operas, none of them will admit it. That's why you're here, because you're so honest!"

With that, the women really started to howl. They laughed and clapped, and I could see that I was doing just what the chaplain had warned me not to do. I definitely had evoked a response. I could see the guards looking more and more concerned, and the chaplain in the back, sort of holding her head, but I could also see the women were really with me. So I kept going and told them that a friend of mine, who was addicted to soap operas, had come across this little piece a few years back, and I thought they'd like to hear it:

AS THE WORLD TURNS, being one of THE YOUNG AND RESTLESS, I spent THE DAYS OF OUR LIVES in a SEARCH FOR TOMORROW that brought me to THE EDGE OF NIGHT. I was headed for ANOTHER WORLD. After winding up in GENERAL HOSPITAL and being cared for by THE DOCTORS, Jesus Christ, THE GUIDING LIGHT, broke through my SECRET STORM. Lovingly He said, "I have rescued you from FALCON CREST: Now share in My DYNASTY, and be one of ALL MY CHILDREN . . . and I will give you ONE LIFE TO LIVE."

By the time I finished, I could just feel the excitement in the air, but then I remembered the chaplain's rules and thought, *Oh, I've done it all wrong . . . I've said the wrong things . . . I shouldn't have mentioned life sentences and no parole. I shouldn't have asked them to raise their hands . . . This is awful . . . I never want to come here again . . . Why did I come? Lord, I shouldn't have come. Why did You make me come?*

I was standing there, feeling as if I were a complete failure, when the girls all stood up and started to file out. But as they passed by me, each one BLEW ME A KISS! What exciting encouragement to me! I hadn't wanted to come and talk in a women's prison. I'd said, "I can't help these women," but my story had encouraged them, and they had refreshed me as well.

The chaplain walked up, and I fully expected to be admonished for what had happened, but instead she said excitedly, "We've never had such a demonstration of love from these women for anybody."

A couple of days later, in the mail came a wonderful note from Chaplain Mrotzek:

Dear Barbara:

Boy—have I been busy! Not because I was behind, but because of the wonderful response from the service.

That is such a wonderful way to be busy! Many rededicated their lives. I had one girl come today to say she was so encouraged and felt so comfortable there. She probably hadn't had much peace in her life. She said, "I'll be there again this Sunday." Hope she's not too disappointed when I preach! The deputies have come and shared how blessed they were, also. See . . . miracles still do happen . . . even the deputies listened!

Several of the girls also wrote me afterward, and I sent them some follow-up material. I thought again about how I'd dragged my feet about going to speak in a prison and then how I'd wished I had never agreed to come. I just hadn't believed I could accomplish much among such "hardened criminals." But God softened their hearts, and because they received encouragement, so did I. In a small way, I had been an Onesiphorus, bringing encouragement into a dark prison where refreshment is as scarce as a smiling face.

How to Be an Onesiphorus

Living like Onesiphorus isn't always easy, but it always pays. In an article on Onesiphorus in *Discipleship Journal* (1986, no. 35), Stephen S. Hopper, a pastor from Grass Valley, California, describes what it takes to be an effective "minister of refreshment." For one thing, you need genuine, *continuing* concern for others. Onesiphorus didn't make just one visit to Paul in prison; he came back again and again. In other words, he followed up. Lots of people say, "Now, if there's anything I can do, just call." Of course, the person who's hurting usually doesn't call, and all too often the one who offered help doesn't check back, either. If you want to be an Onesiphorus, you don't wait for friends in need to call—you call them!

To be an Onesiphorus, you're going to have to be persistent. Onesiphorus searched hard for Paul until he found him. (See 2 Timothy 1:17.) He didn't wait until he had some free time or until he was "in the neighborhood." He kept going the extra mile until he could bring refreshment and encouragement.

Opportunities to refresh and encourage others are everywhere. Surely you know someone who is . . .

- In an unfamiliar situation, like a new job, or possibly away at school.
- Tired and weary of it all.
- Lonely, and wondering if anybody cares any more.
- Experiencing disappointment or discouragement.
- Uncertain of the future because of poor health, job setbacks, or any number of other reasons.
- Under tremendous stress, pressure, or pain.

If someone's name or face flashes to mind, stop right now and make plans about how you will be Onesiphorus for that person in the next few days, or maybe the next few minutes. I get lots of letters that tell me it's worth it. One of the most special ones said:

Dear Barb,

I just had to share with you how God used your September newsletter to minister to me. September 29 my doctor called to tell me, very unexpectedly, that the mole he had removed was malignant. I had a rare, high-risk melanoma and would need more surgery. I hung up the phone, sat down at the kitchen table, and there on top of the stack of unopened mail was the September Spatula newsletter. My eyes fell on the cartoon of the lady tied to the railroad tracks with "I don't recall asking for any of this." I burst out laughing and turned my face to my heavenly Father and said, "Lord, how true!" What a wonderful sense of timing and humor the Lord has. That little cartoon made a tense moment bearable.

I had not asked God for the daily heartache that our 2 (out of 4) rebellious children have caused—but His sustaining grace has been sufficient for each day. I had not asked Him for our (4½-year-old) cerebral palsy grandson that we are raising—but God made him a precious, loving sunbeam who's taught me much of His loving heart. And I had not asked God for this cancer, but I knew He was going to go through this experience with me—and He has. The doctor "got it all," the skin graft took, and I'm mending daily without fear of the future.

Thanks for your ministry that meets us in a variety of needs where we are hurting and brings smiles to our hearts.

It's true that none of us can recall that we've asked for what life has brought us. But we can reach out to others and encourage them in the midst of whatever seems to be bearing down on them (or what has already run over them!). And as we do, we will *always* be encouraged as well.

One of God's Proverbs says: "Anxiety in a man's heart weighs him down, but a good word makes him glad" (Proverbs 12:25, RSV). After years of helping me encourage others, God finally sent "that good word," and I'll share what it was in the next—and last—chapter.

Extra Thoughts to Take Along

THE MINISTRY OF LETTERS

Lord, sometimes I think
I can't strike another typewriter key.
I can't write another paragraph or word.
I can't even put a period
At the end of a sentence.
I look at the fat bundle
Of unanswered letters
And it all seems so futile
So time-consuming, so unending.
I can't think or concentrate.
What I write seems empty, lifeless.
I struggle to keep my thoughts coherent.

Yet, I know I must keep on.
I have committed myself
To a ministry of writing—
Writing letters!

And often, God, when I begin to question
My personal commitment
You send me a ray of hope . . .
A personal rainbow.
Someone stops me to say
"Ten years ago, when I needed it most,
You sent me a letter of encouragement.
I've read it a hundred times.
It's worn and tear-stained
But I'll treasure it forever."

Lord, I don't even remember writing.
It's been so long.
But it doesn't matter.
I see again the value of ministry
And so I'll continue.
But first, Lord I must put a period after the sentence
I so wearily wrote just an hour ago.

—Ruth Harms Calkin

* * * *

OATMEAL DAYS

It's not always the red-flag crisis days that are hardest to take. It's the "oatmeal days." The ordinary, "zero" days of little or no consequence. The ho-hum days filled with nothing of any particular interest. Colorless. Uninteresting. Unfascinating. Unspectacular. And unfun. The days everyone deals with.

We cope. We wend our way through the tangle of tedious activity and sandpaper people scattered through our day and get no applause, because coping is expected.

Not so during the red-flag crisis times. People tend to rally behind us with loving support. We're lifted above the crisis and enabled beyond human comprehension at times.

On oatmeal days, after a crisis has peaked, it may seem as if friends have forsaken us, as if God doesn't care. But the reality will be that life has merely pushed us and our friends one step further in the Christian growth-walk.

The God of the crisis times is the God of the oatmeal days, too. Because He said He is. Because He keeps His promises—always. Because we can't get along without Him. And because we wouldn't want to if we could.

—Source Unknown

11

My Future's So Bright
I Gotta Wear Shades

When dreams come true at last, there is life and joy.

—Proverbs 13:12, TLB

It was an extra busy Monday, early in May 1986. I had spent the prior weekend speaking at a three-day women's conference sponsored by Campus Crusade in Arrowhead Springs, California. Now I was back home, hurriedly getting ready to leave again almost immediately for an extended trip to Minnesota, where I would speak at the Billy Graham Evangelistic Association chapel plus several Mother's Day banquets in churches in the Minneapolis area.

The trip meant being gone for Mother's Day, but that didn't seem to matter a great deal. Barney and his family were going to drop by before we left to wish me a happy Mother's Day, and Larry . . . well, Larry hadn't called for five Mother's Days in a row. He had been gone without a word or trace since January 1980, so I was getting used to it—or so I thought.

And then, as I was packing and going over notes of talks I would give to parents on how we all have to give our kids to God and leave the results up to Him because God never gives the score on a life until the game is over, the telephone rang!

It was Larry! The voice I had longed to hear for so many years said, "I want to come over and give you a Mother's Day present."

What a shock! I froze with apprehension! My first thought

was, *Why now? Why does he want to bring me a present? I bet he's going to tell me he's going to marry his lover . . . or that he has AIDS.*

I just didn't know what to say, so I stammered, "Well, Larry, I don't know, I'm so busy getting ready to leave for a big trip . . . lots of speaking engagements . . . not sure we've got time . . . just a minute, let me talk to Dad . . ."

When I look back on this conversation, I can see the irony, but at that moment, I was confused, stalling for time. For six years I had been speaking to groups all over the country, telling parents to hang in there, that God would bring their wayward children back from the "far country," and now my *own son* was finally on the line, and I was telling him I was TOO BUSY to see him because I was leaving to go speak about having hope and joy when your kids disappoint you!

I put my hand over the receiver and said to Bill, "It's Larry! He wants to come over and give me a Mother's Day present. I'm not sure I should let him come . . . what if he wants to tell us he's marrying his lover . . . or something even worse?"

Mr. Wumphee just looked at me and said unhesitatingly, "You have him come home!"

I could see Bill wasn't going to do anything to get me off the hook, so trying my best to sound light and happy, I told Larry, "Okay . . . you can come over."

The next hour seemed to drag by. Larry had said he was about fifty miles away, but I kept wondering if he would really come. And then I wondered if it were all a bad dream. I could talk a good game to other parents, but now it was my turn to see if I could really cut the mustard! It was all too good (or maybe bad) to be true!

When the doorbell rang, I almost jumped. How could he be here that SOON? I opened the door, and there was Larry, standing tall, with a clear-eyed look I hadn't seen for eleven years. But he had no present in his hand, and my heart sank. He had come to give me some kind of news for a gift, and what would that news be? Would it leave me counting roses on the wallpaper again? I invited him in, cautiously, with only a perfunctory little hug—wondering if I should remark about the absent present. As we sat down in the living room, I could see big tears in his eyes, and then I heard his words:

"I want you to forgive me for the eleven years of pain I have caused you. Last week I went to an advanced seminar for Basic Youth Conflicts, and I . . . I rededicated my life to the Lord. I took all the evidence of the old life, the pictures and everything else to do with the lifestyle—everything—I took it to a fireplace and, while the whole thing was burning, I felt this complete release for the first time in eleven years. I'm released from that bondage I was in, and God has really cleansed me. Now I can stand clean before the Lord."

What a glorious Mother's Day present! A gift wrapped in LOVE!

And then Larry gave us a little bonus with news about the young man he had been living with. The night after Larry got his life right with the Lord, his friend went forward at the Basic Youth seminar and received Christ as Savior.

This young man was a brand-new Christian, and my son had rededicated his life to the Lord! We sat there for a long time and just hugged each other. He had asked for our forgiveness, and we needed his forgiveness as well for our failures to understand his hurts. We were overjoyed to have him back again, and that day a restoration began in our family that is continuing even now.

Joy Washed over Me

Larry stayed for over two hours, and we laughed and cried and hugged and shared. For years I had been talking about having joy and how joy is like God living in the marrow of your bones. Now joy was washing over me in huge waves! All the verses I had been quoting to other parents now sang praises in my own heart.

"Hope deferred makes the heart sick; but when dreams come true at last, there is life and joy" (Proverbs 13:12, TLB). Hope had been deferred for me for eleven years. Ever since that night at the flagpole at Disneyland in 1975, I had hoped and prayed, but my heart had been heavy. I had found joy where I could; I had

refused to let misery overwhelm me, but now I felt life and joy in every cell of my body.

"'*There is hope for your future,' declares the* LORD. '*Your children will return to their own land*'" (Jeremiah 31:17, NIV). For eleven years, I had hoped and prayed that Larry would return to the Lord. Promises like this one were the only thing that gave me any real hope. And now he had "come back to his own land" after wandering in the gay lifestyle.

"*I will . . . transform her Valley of Troubles into a Door of Hope*" (Hosea 2:15, TLB). God had not only transformed my "valley of troubles" into a door of hope. He had thrown open wide that door and Larry had walked through it back into our lives!

"*And you can . . . be very sure that God will rescue the children of the godly*" (Proverbs 11:21, TLB). What a promise for Christians who realize their righteousness, or godliness, comes only through believing in Jesus Christ! God had rescued my child. Our fractured relationship was being healed.

We left the next day for Minneapolis, where we planned to stay with my sister, Janet, and her husband, Mel, who is a radio minister and evangelist there. I was sure I could have flown there with my own wings, but Bill convinced me we should take a jet. I told Bill not to tell them about Larry's return because I wanted to save it for a surprise when I spoke at a banquet scheduled at their church that next evening. But when we arrived and Janet picked us up at the airport, Bill couldn't contain himself and blurted out, "Barb has a secret, but she's not going to tell you until later."

Of course, Janet wouldn't quit until she wheedled it out of me. And when I told her Larry had returned and asked for forgiveness, she wept with joy. Mel's reaction was to excitedly schedule me to be on his radio broadcast the next morning so he could have a scoop before I told about Larry at the banquet.

The next night at the banquet, which had a Mother's Day theme, I shared about Larry's return and the total peace and joy that Bill and I had for the first time since our long, eleven-year parenthesis of pain began in 1975. I explained that after Larry had returned the first time, we had lived in a sort of vacuum, not really mentioning his problem and "assuming" everything was all right. Before he left the second time, he had thrown the Bible in our faces and disowned us. Now, after a total of eleven years, God had kicked the end out of our parenthesis, and we were free!

The reaction to my news was dramatic—lots of tears, smiles, and even applause. Every mom in the room identified with my joy, and one mother, who had wanted to die after recently learning that her son was gay, got up and shared how she now had new hope because of what had happened with Larry.

Faith Is My Distant Cousin

I spoke several more times that Mother's Day weekend before returning home and setting off again to encourage some SPATULA cluster groups in the Seattle area with our wonderful news. *The Love Line* newsletter for July 1986 was a special one, dedicated to sharing the news of Larry's return.

Larry even contributed to that newsletter. He wrote all of our SPATULA friends and said:

> My mother has told me of the countless people who have prayed for me these many years. Praise God for His faithfulness!
>
> I'm sure many of you wonder what it was that brought such a change in my life. All I can say, briefly, is that when I attended a Basic Youth Seminar, taught by Bill Gothard, I discovered the victory that we have in Christ and the power to be free from moral impurity and bitterness.
>
> There have been many changes for me these past weeks since I rededicated my life to Christ. I can only say that I am truly thankful that God, in His mercy, has forgiven me and I look forward to being of service to Him.

That issue of *The Love Line* also included a congratulatory note penned personally by Dr. James Dobson a couple of months before. As you can see, he got so excited, he ran out of space:

That newsletter generated a large amount of mail as many Spatulanders wrote to express their joy for me. But while all this speaking and writing about Larry's return was going on, I had a reaction that left me with the old doubts and fears. What if Larry suddenly slipped back into the old lifestyle? After all, there was so much residue from all those years of living in rebellion and sin. How long does it take to have a renewing of the mind? I just didn't know.

When Jim Dobson called and invited me to be on his "Focus on the Family" radio show to talk about Larry, I hesitated at

first. I wondered if I was ready to go on national radio or television and share all this with the "whole world." Perhaps I
should wait until some time had elapsed—to be sure Larry
was really out of the gay lifestyle for good.

Larry had returned, and I was overjoyed that he had asked
forgiveness and that being forgiven was so important to him.
That was crucial in my mind because I knew God would work
from that foundation. It would take time to know for sure if
his contrition and tears would last. I guess I'm not a woman
of a lot of faith. For me joy and hope go together; they're sis-
ters. But faith is sort of a distant cousin for me. I've been told
I have the gift of joy, but faith hasn't been my gift, so I borrow
it from others who have plenty to spare.

Larry and I Made a Tape Together

But as the weeks went by, my fears subsided, and I agreed
to go on Dr. Dobson's program in October.

Just before doing the "Focus on the Family" broadcast, I
made a tape with Larry to share with just the Spatula family.
We met in his apartment, high above sprawling downtown
Los Angeles, and shared our thoughts about what had happened and how we felt now that he had been back for several
months.

On that tape he shared what had brought about his change.
Obviously, guilt had dogged his footsteps for eleven years, and
he had longed to have his relationship to us restored. Then he
attended the Advanced Basic Youth Conflicts Seminar led by
Bill Gothard, and all of the principles and values he had so vio-
lently rejected eleven years ago had taken root in a new and
wonderful way. As Larry said, "God either gives us the grace
to overcome these things, or we become embittered. And I
think Basic Youth Conflicts taught me how to overcome that
bitterness and be able to enjoy the grace of God again."

Larry also talked about how important it was to ask his parents' forgiveness. He learned a very important principle: "If
you can't respond to your parents properly, you can't respond
to other people properly."

We also shared a great deal about our failures—his and mine. If there is anything the homosexual child needs when his parents learn of his orientation, it's unconditional love. But unconditional love is very hard to give in those first moments of being totally devastated and emotionally overwrought.

Larry quoted a Psalm that promises, "The LORD is near to those who have a broken heart, and saves such as have a contrite spirit" (Psalm 34:18, NKJV). And then he said, "We all have failures, in whatever area is in our lives, but it really is important that we understand we must acknowledge those failures to the people whom we have failed and try to bring about restoration in our lives. . . . That's the miracle of the power that Christ gives us . . . to be able to transform failures into victories."

As our interview went on, I told Larry how wonderful it is to start out the day and know the past is over and that he doesn't have to live in bondage to the unhappy memories of the past and I don't have to, either.

"That's because we've been able to forgive each other," Larry replied. "Forgiveness is a very powerful thing—the ability to forgive and the ability to be forgiven. When someone comes to you and says, 'I was wrong in what I did to you; will you forgive me?' that's a very powerful thing . . . because it releases a burden of guilt. . . . What holds people back from doing that is their own pride, their own inability to say, 'I made a mistake; I was wrong.' Now, a lot of parents don't want to do that, but when a child sees the parent not willing to admit his mistakes, what makes you think the child would want to admit his own?"

As we talked, Larry recalled how our own relationship had been strained to the point of total destruction when I first learned of his homosexuality. "Some of the things that you said were terrible," he remembered. "Reckless words, like a piercing sword."

I remembered those devastating moments, too. On that shocking Sunday afternoon, I had said I would have preferred Larry's being dead to his being gay. That's why I tell people to shove a sock in their mouth and to not say anything for six months, or they'll say the wrong thing because they're in such a state of panic—completely unglued.

As Larry and I continued our discussion, I asked him what a parent should do if a child calls to say he has AIDS—how should parents deal with this? His answer pointed toward the only real hope anyone has in this fallen world. He said:

"Parents should remember that they're Christians, and that we do worship a God of deliverance, not of death. God wants to supernaturally reveal Himself to the world, and the only way He can do that is through Christians—through the people who love Him and worship Him. We live in terrifying times, but as Christians we have power over death and over sin, just as Christ did."

As we closed our interview, I asked Larry what the future held for him. He had gotten his life right before God and planned to serve the Lord. What did he think God had in mind for his life? He answered, "All I know is that if I purpose in my heart to be loving in everything I do, the Lord will open up those things for me, and I'm confident in that. I know that as long as I'm in His Word and doing what He feels is right, and I'm joyful and thankful for everything that He has given to me, I don't have to fear the future."

That interview with Larry made my heart smile, and I was able to do the radio program with Dr. James Dobson a few days later with confident joy. At one point I said to Dr. Dobson and the radio audience, "We're on this journey to becoming whole; the ones that are farther down the road can reach back and pull the other ones along. That's how it's supposed to be."

He interrupted me and asked, "Do you mean to tell me there may come a day when a parent could reach out and help somebody else?"

"I guarantee that," I told the radio listeners. "After a few months of walking in this tunnel, you're going to see a light at the other end, and it *won't* be another train coming. That light is going to be God's love and God's light on you, and as you go through this and you begin to heal, those raw edges are going to be healed by God's love and you're going to reach back and find another person who is where you are now. That's the whole purpose of this ministry—being able to pull the ones up that are in that deep tunnel and pull them through. We've seen it happen hundreds of times!"

New Joy Gave Us New Energy

Larry's return, not only to us but more importantly to the Lord, spurred us on to continue working with even more diligence to help pull parents through their long, dark tunnel of despair. Their letters continued to pour in, and one mom's words particularly grabbed my heart because she told of not *one* son who had declared he was homosexual, but *two*:

Dear Barb:

When my two sons (twins) told me two months ago that they were homosexual, I wanted to die. Really die! I considered suicide but was too chicken. I was sad, angry, and hurt, and so very confused. Where had we gone wrong? We had sent them to Christian schools. They went to church, had good Christian friends. What had happened? The only thing I could think of was to call a friend long distance. I did just that, and thank God, I did. She told me she was sending a book. About three days later it arrived: *Where Does a Mother Go to Resign?*

My head was like stone. I could not concentrate to read it. My wonderful husband began to read it to me. As he began to read, I realized I was not alone.

That book saved my life. Every feeling you expressed I was feeling at that time. I began slowly to come alive. Our sons were hurting also. We began talking openly about the problem. I loved them so very much. We all cried together. They are *special* young men, and I feel our Lord has something great in store for them.

I know now, as you said, the only two things we can do is pray for them and love them. . . . Yes, there are still difficult days but I'm learning to put things in Jesus' hands. . . . Keep up the great work!

In twelve years of helping parents, I had never heard from anyone who had twins who were gay. This mother's pain was double, but she was climbing out of her pit by using two of the most important principles any parent needs when a child goes into the gay lifestyle, alcoholism, drug addiction, sexual perversion, and any number of other terrible problems that can afflict a family. These concepts almost sound contradictory, but in reality they work together to bring about change and healing.

- Love your child unconditionally.

- Let your child go—release him to God's care.

I would like to meet the mother of the prodigal son. I wonder where she was when her son was slopping the hogs and living in the pigpen. (She probably was in a home for the bewildered.) What was she doing when they were preparing the feast for his homecoming?

Unconditional Love Is Not "Sloppy Agape"

I'm often asked during interviews and talk shows just HOW can a parent show "unconditional love." One lady wondered if it meant just loving everyone and "letting them do their own thing." My answer was that that would be "sloppy agape" love that had no real substance or toughness. The point is, we may not always love what our children are doing—their lifestyle and values—but we love *them*!

Unconditional love does not mean that you cannot have rules concerning what your child can or cannot do within the family. I don't believe Scripture teaches that we should let the sin of one person destroy everyone else. For example, if the child is coming in drunk or on drugs, you can't let that disrupt the rest of the family. Recently, I picked up a saying that I like a great deal:

*THE MAIN THING IS TO KEEP
THE MAIN THING THE MAIN THING.*

When your child is in trouble, the main thing is to keep your relationship to God and your spouse and the others in your family solid while you continue to reach out to the one who's wandering. You have to say, "Hey, I love you, but I love you so much that I can't let you destroy the family. You're going to have to find another place. We'll help you."

If possible, get your child out on his own if he's over eighteen and able to hold a job. Support and love your child in every legitimate way you can, but do not support the sin that has him in its grasp. You want your child to know that home is a loving, warm, comfortable place, but it is not an incubator for immature behavior. Don't fur-line the pigpen for your child when he should be on his own.

If your child is younger (under eighteen), remember that you are still in charge of your home. You can still make the rules, and I repeat, you can have rules for your home and still have unconditional love for a rebellious child. You can set limits, lock doors, and throw out stuff that you don't want there. You don't have to have someone in your home doing things there that you don't want them to be doing and scattering all that pain and all that sin all over the house.

All this advice sounds simple, but I realize it is not easy to practice. The trick is to be firm in holding to your standards but at the same time to show your child unconditional love and compassion. In my experience, I found that unconditional love comes only out of constant prayer. "Praying about it" is often held out as the great Christian answer to everything, as if God will magically solve all problems if we just say our prayers often enough. I don't believe that, but I do believe prayer is the foundation to answering whatever is tearing and ripping at your family. It brings the security you crave.

Security Blanket

When you were my beloved baby,
I wrapped you in a blanket—
In your precious "dee-dee"—
Thankful you were content for the moment.

Now you are grown and far away,
And I wrap you in prayer—
In our precious Savior's promises—
Thankful you are safe and secure for eternity.

                                        —*Ann Luna*

Never Stop Loving Your Child

The late Joseph Bayly, who wrote many fine Christian books and articles over his long career, once shared his heart about the "rebel" in his own family. He had one boy out of a total of five children who decided to rebel over a four- or five-year period from the late teens to early twenties. After one year at Bible college, the son declared his independence, cut all ties, and hitch-hiked across the country to live his own life on the West Coast.

With his son living half a continent away, Joseph Bayly became depressed, but his wife, Mary Lou, said, "We must pray all the more. *We're* not in San Diego with our son, but God is."

What is prayer but turning to God? And nothing can turn a parent to God more quickly than a wayward child. After all, when a child rebels and is utterly out of control, where else can you turn? And it's times like that when you have the chance to grow in faith. I have to admit, however, that I'm better at hope and joy than I am at faith.

Joseph Bayly also posed a very thought-provoking question: "Does faith really mean much unless it is tested, unless it is exercised in the darkness?" To answer his own question, he refers to Hebrews 11:1: "Now faith is the substance of things hoped for, the evidence of things not seen" (NKJV).

Bayly went on to say that God does not disown you or me when we rebel against Him. Rather "He always is there, waiting with outstretched arms for us to return. He is the waiting Father." Likewise, "we must be waiting parents, with arms and love extended. Even if years of disappointment and anxiety pass in the meantime."

To Love Your Child . . . Let Go

It sounds confusing to some parents, but to unconditionally love your child, *no matter what*, you also have to LET THAT

CHILD GO. How can you love your child and let him go at the same time? The answer: *Give him to God!*

Parents ask me over and over: "How can I give my child to God?" I explain how I did it that day I said, "Whatever, Lord," but many parents are in such emotional turmoil they need some kind of illustration to help. I found such an illustration recently, something that can perhaps help you mentally give your child to God's care.

Picture in your mind that you are placing your daughter or son in a gift box. Then wrap the box with lovely paper and a ribbon. Next, imagine the glorious throne of God, which is at the top of a long flight of stairs. Picture yourself walking up those stairs, carrying your lovely gift-wrapped package.

Put your package down at the feet of Jesus, who is sitting on the throne. Wait there as He bends down, picks up the package, and puts it on His lap. Then He will remove the wrappings, take off the lid, and lift your child out.

Watch as Jesus wraps the child in His loving arms and holds him close. After you see Jesus holding him, you walk back down the stairs, pausing partway down to look back to reassure yourself that Jesus still has your child in His arms. Then you continue down the stairs, thanking God for taking control.

You have given your prodigal to God. He or she is no longer in your hands. Now you are ready to ask God to do whatever is necessary to help your child. You may have to see circumstances that seem to tear you apart, but God will undertake to reach your rebel, often in very dramatic ways. Whenever you are tempted to take control again, you must practice this little thought exercise. Remember the specific time when you presented your child as a gift to the Lord and He received him in faithful love.

I'm not saying this will be easy. The old cliché says, "Let go and let God," but letting go is always the hardest part. Once we let go, then it's easier to let God do what He's ready to do.

During those years when Larry was gone, particularly his

second absence, I would speak to various groups, and people would ask, "How is your family *now?*"

I would reply, "Well, my two sons haven't risen from the dead and my third son is still out there in the gay life."

"Well, how can you be so happy and have such joy?" people wanted to know.

And my answer was always the same: "It's because I've given it to the Lord. I've said, 'Whatever, Lord.' I've relinquished it to the Lord, and I've got a life to get busy with living."

Conviction from God Makes the Difference

If we're going "to let go and let God," we must fear less and trust in Christ more. I'm often asked if homosexuals can completely change. Many Christians believe homosexuality is like any other sin—that it's a matter of choice and all the homosexual has to do is "get right with God" and his orientation will become heterosexual.

Over the past years, I have met hundreds of homosexual young men, many of whom are Christians. I love these kids and believe that most of them don't want their homosexual feelings. They didn't ask for this. I don't think anybody would ask to be a homosexual because there is so much animosity and rejection. But for some reason that even the experts don't understand, something has happened at the core of their personality.

Although no one really knows what causes homosexuality, many believe this phenomenon could be brought about by any number of things. However, to suggest that there might be various causes for homosexuality does not mean that the Christian can approve of homosexual behavior.

It's not wrong to have homosexual feelings; the wrong comes in *acting out* the homosexual lifestyle. There are those who have homosexual feelings, but they don't ever act on them. They live their lives, realizing they have a very vulnerable area with which they're always going to have to struggle—just as we all have areas of our lives where we are more vulnerable than others. But I believe God will give us all, even the homosexual, the grace to live a clean life and to stand clean before the Lord.

Most of the homosexuals that I'm talking about have had Christian parents who tried to raise them right, and those parents just don't understand what happened. I don't understand, either. As we read in the book of Deuteronomy, "The secret things belong to the LORD" (Deuteronomy 29:29, RSV). Most of these young men would never have chosen homosexuality, but for some reason, something got scrambled and didn't come out as it should have—something like a flower that didn't open. Instead of opening correctly, their sexuality became inverted. No one is at fault; it just happened.

With some good counseling and with love from their parents, their family, and their church, I believe homosexuals can live a clean life without acting out their orientation. However, a shift in behavior may depend on the person's motivation and the depth of his commitment to the gay lifestyle.

We know that the homosexual lifestyle is a real entrenching behavior. But we can't put God in a box and say He has to heal everybody in a certain way. You can't say that a person is only effective as a Christian when he's married and has a family. I just know that God has touched my son's life. He's clean before the Lord, and it's exciting to see what God is going to do in his life. And whatever happens, we know that it has to be God's touch in his life. Healing always has to be of God. It has to be God's touch in any area, whether it's alcohol, drugs, or whatever. Condemnation will not bring change. It is only conviction from God that brings a shift in behavior.

Why the Future Is So Bright

The title of this chapter comes from a bumper sticker a friend found and sent me because it reminded her of me. But what it reminds me of is what Larry said when we made that tape together in 1986. His exact words were, "I don't have any fear for the future." I don't, either, because the future is now bright with God's hope and love.

You may be thinking, *"That's fine for you, Barbara. Your*

child is back and living a clean life, but mine is still out there, wandering alone in a lifestyle that can destroy him." I understand. That's why I wrote yet another book, to let you know THERE IS HOPE.

God can take your trouble and change it into treasure. Your sorrow can be exchanged for joy, not just a momentary smile, but a deep new joy. It will be a bubbling experience of new hope that brings brightness to your eyes and a song to your heart. In the midst of the darkness, you will learn lessons you might never have learned in the day. We all have seen dreams turn to ashes—ugly things, hopeless and heartbreaking—but beauty for ashes is God's exchange.

Tears and sorrow come, but each time God will be there to remind you that He cares. Romans 8:28 means that God causes all things in our lives to work together for good. Flowers can even grow on dung hills, and compost makes great gardens. God is offering Himself to you daily, and the rate of exchange is fixed. It is your sins for His forgiveness, your tragedy and hurt for His balm of healing, and your sorrow for His joy.

Give God the pain and sorrow; give Him the guilt you feel. Tears and heartaches come to us all. They are part of living, but Jesus Christ can ease the heartache.

Remember, you are not alone; many are in God's waiting room for what seems like forever, learning lessons, suffering pain, and growing. But the fertilizer that helps us grow is in those valleys, not on the mountaintops.

The iron crown of suffering precedes the golden crown of glory. So give your child to God and then focus on getting your own life together. Also keep in mind that you *are not responsible for what you cannot control* and that God has only called you to be *faithful*. He did not call you to be *successful!*

Real genuine healing is a process. It takes a long, long time for the deep hurts to be resolved. Sometimes it seems that they will be with us forever, but understanding them helps dissipate their pain.

Life isn't always what you want, but it's what you've got; so, with God's help, CHOOSE TO BE HAPPY—and He will see you and your loved ones home safe at last!

🌼 A Final Thought to Take Along 🌼

HE'LL SEE THEM HOME

Don't despair so of your children,
God will bring them to the fold—
Because He died to save them,
They're special to the Lord.
He knows how much you love them,
He loves them even more.
As long as you hold on in prayer,
He'll not close the door.
Even now He sees your tears,
And He whispers tenderly,
Of love that conquered all—
That all men might be free.

So lay them at His altar,
Let go and leave them there—
God will be faithful to your trust,
He won't withhold His care.
His hand will ever nurture,
No matter where they roam—
And He won't be satisfied
'Til He sees them safely home!

—Joyce Henning

Notes

Chapter 1. Pain Is Inevitable, But Misery Is Optional
1. Ashleigh Brilliant, *Pot-Shots* No. 1318, © Brilliant Enterprises 1977. Used by permission.

Chapter 5. One Laugh = 3 Tbsp. Oat Bran
1. Josleen Wilson, *The Oat Bran Way* (New York: Berkley Books, 1989), 71, 72.
2. On California highways, the Diamond Lane is reserved for cars with two or more people who are commuting together.

Chapter 6. Guilt—The Gift That Keeps on Giving
1. © 1987 Remarkable Things, Long Beach, Calif. Used by permission of Larry Thomas.

Chapter 8. I Married Mr. Wumphee
1. The best description of temperaments I've heard and seen comes from Florence Littauer, who has published a set of cassette tapes on temperaments, as well as the book *Personality Plus* (Old Tappan, N.J.: Fleming H. Revell, 1983).

More joy from the
Geranium Lady!

God's Most Precious Jewels are Crystallized Tears contains the stories of twelve extraordinary women as they journeyed through incredible hardship to become sparkling jewels of joy and encouragement to others. Barbara includes her own story of grief turned to blessing with her signature touch of hope and humor. Woven throughout these inspiring stories are descriptions of real gemstones—their origin and their traditional meanings.

If you need a fresh breath of joy in your life, Barbara's 365-day devotional will help you look for life's little sparkles, even in the midst of life's most crippling sorrows. Love and hilarity bubble through these pages in equal doses as Barbara dispenses her unique blend of wisdom and zaniness to help thousands of hurting readers learn to laugh again. Each day's devotion features a Scripture passage and encouraging thought all wrapped up in Barbara's trademark style of offering firsthand advice about handling life's hardest hurts while dispensing infectious laughter and outrageous joy.

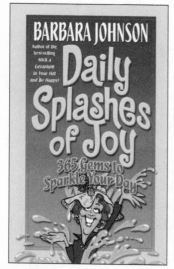

PUBLISHING GROUP™

Bad news about your children carries a triple whammy of pain, worry, and "where did we go wrong?" Drawing on her own personal experience and the letters she has received from hundreds of hurting women, Barbara shares hope and humor to encourage parents in seemingly hopeless situations.

Barbara Johnson combines fun and inspiration in a pick-me-up book that's chocked full of her patented wit and wisdom, love and laughter, and comfort and grace. A primer for those new to Barbara's message of hope, *Humor Me* is a must-have addition to one's current library of Geranium Lady books. This "best of" collection contains sidesplitting jokes, one-liners worth remembering, silly stories, and chuckle-worthy cartoons on topics such as men, parenting, and aging.

Barbara insists that laughing in the face of adversity is not a form of denial but a proven tool for managing stress, coping with pain, and maintaining hope. She zeroes in on the spiritual benefit of a smile, a giggle, and a good, old-fashioned belly laugh.

PUBLISHING GROUP™

For women only, this is one of Barbara's most unique books. With her zany collection of observations about "life between the Blue Lagoon and Golden Pond," Barbara jumps right in, showing women how to survive growing older with courage and joy.

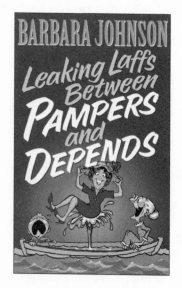

Between the years of childbearing and grandparenting, a woman has a lot to juggle! Barbara Johnson shows how the road from marriage to menopause is filled with more than a few potholes . . . but provides women with more than enough hope and humor to make it through the journey.

Pack Up Your Gloomees is filled with bittersweet stories of Barbara's journey through the minefields of life and her wise and encouraging responses to letters from hurting parents. Each chapter ends with a laughter-packed collection of Gloomee Busters.

 PUBLISHING GROUP™

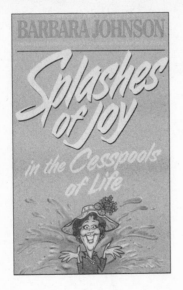

Barbara's approach to life is positive, uplifting, therapeutic and fun. *Splashes of Joy* offers an invigorating spurt of encouragement and a gentle reminder to splatter joy into the lives of others.

Sharing outrageous humor, rib-tickling insights, and inspiring, real-life examples, Barbara shows readers how to put life's trials into heavenly perspective. While we wait on Gabriel's horn to sound, Barbara gives women an external telescope with which to view their often difficult world.

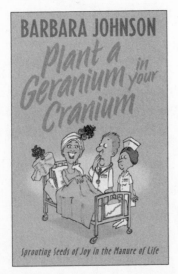

Best-selling humorist Barbara Johnson is back—and getting back to her roots—with a candid look at life and discovering joy in the midst of trials, including her own unexpected battle with cancer. Using excerpts from inspiring articles and extraordinary letters from her mailbag, Johnson presents one big package of humor, comfort, and encouragement that her beloved audiences have come to expect.

Ⓦ PUBLISHING GROUP™